Hiding in Plain Sight

Sabbath Blessings

Molly Wolf

A Liturgical Press Book

THE LITURGICAL PRESS
Collegeville, Minnesota

Cover design by Ann Blattner. Embroidery by Molly Wolf.

Printed in the United States of America.

1	2	3	4	5	6	7	8	9

Library of Congress Cataloging-in-Publication Data

Wolf, Molly, 1949–
    Hiding in plain sight : Sabbath blessings / Molly Wolf.
      p.   cm.
    ISBN 0-8146-2506-1 (alk. paper)
    1. Meditations.   I. Title.
BL624.2.W65   1998
242—dc21   98-5162
                                                      CIP

Learn what you must learn,
Go where you must go;
When you stop running, stand still,
Listen, you will know
That you can find God where you are
Hiding in plain sight.

Deborah Griffin Bly

Contents

Preface: Hiding in Plain Sight

All too often, it seems to me, religious writing falls into the abstruse ("Dr. Schrenk's exegesis of the Pauline texts, while based firmly in a subject-subject analysis of the eschatological subtext, is not unfraught with ontological ambiguities") or the unreal ("My husband left me for my sister's boyfriend, and the dog has both hips in a cast, but I count it all joy, *joy,* JOY!!!"). The first of these awakens in me an overwhelming urge to go clean the refrigerator. The second reminds me strongly of grinding car gears—I don't know why, but there it is. Maybe God is in this stuff, too, but I can't make sense of the God in question. If I do my own writing instead, it's to make sense of God for myself, to see where God lurks in my life.

In 1995 I found myself starting to write pieces each Saturday (hence the subtitle of this book) for two Internet Anglican mailing lists—one Canadian and one international. It seemed natural to ground my weekly bits in whatever was going on, more or less. I didn't want to always talk about what was really happening in my life; these pieces, while personal, are not, I hope, too confessional. But I do find it easier to relate God-talk to the practical, the everyday, the here-and-now. And I do try to be honest. I can't "solve" the problem of evil; I can only try to look at the spider from the spider's point of view. (An acquaintance with biology helps.)

My sister-in-the-Spirit, Deb Bly, a member of the group Miserable Offenders, wrote a song called "Where You Are," which talks about finding God "hiding in plain sight." (from the compact disc *God Help Us,* Harrisburg, Pa.: Morehouse Publishing, 1996). And that indeed is where God is: not locked in the tabernacle, not hiding behind a mass of complex, eye-crossing philosophical concepts, not absent from our pain, not Out There Somewhere, not running the universe like a clockwork automaton, but here with us, in us, between and among us, in the laundry, the scutwork, the landscape we walk through. If God seems to be hiding, it's likely because of our own failure to notice what God's up to, and this probably says a lot about us but not much about God.

Maybe for some people this is too trivial, too mundane, too ordinary a way of looking at God. If so, there are plenty of other and better Christian writers. But I have indeed "found love, found joy, found God" where I am "hiding in plain sight." And I can only write about what I know.

I could not have written these pieces without the support of my beloved cyberparish, St. Sam's, otherwise known as the Anglican Mailing List, which has held and supported me through Interesting Times. Allen Stairs, whose poem "holy Saturday" appears herein, gave me the needed push to start putting a manuscript together; for that, and for his invaluable love and support through some very dark periods, I thank him with all my heart. I thank my mother, Barbara Wolf, for being my personal theological trainer, always ready to talk through a concept and correct me when I get off course. I thank Linda Maloney and the good people at The Liturgical Press for taking a chance on an unknown author. I thank all from whom I have learned, often the extremely hard way.

Blessings on my father, ✠Fred Wolf, and sisters in the Spirit and the flesh, Deb, Caro, Cynthia, Jane, and Julie; on Jim and my "other children," the Jungs; on Peter and the others at Gordon; on Brian Reid and Bob Chandler, who run the Internet lists I write for; on St. Sam's and all who dwell therein, even Bearded Bill; on the little town I live in that keeps my roots fed and watered, my good neighbors; on both parishes of St. James, with special hugs for Frank.

Thanks above all to the One who made me and loves me and keeps me going and is patient while I struggle to understand. "Breathe on me, Breath of God . . ."

This book is for my kids, Ross and John Greenough, and for a bloke called Henry.

Part 1

God Among the Dandelions

-1-

Herbs of Grace

The Rich Folks' Yard

Typical Saturday: hit the ground running and keep running until somehow it all gets done. Or most of it gets done. Or at least the bits I *can* get done get done, and the rest I'll get around to later, I hope . . .

To the city to drop off a child and run some necessary errands. At one point in a great deal of running around, the most intelligent way to get from Point A to Point B in the inevitable tearing hurry was to take the parkway through The Rich Folks' Yard, the area of the city where live the Mandarins and Ambassadors and People in High Places and People with Lots and Lots of Money. It's a very handsome area, and the parkway that winds through it is both scenic and great fun to drive. But what gave me the giggles, what made my morning, in fact, was the realization that this area had the same—I don't know if you'd call it a *problem* exactly; more a condition, like dandruff—as my lowly unmowed back yard and every roadside and field I had passed this morning.

Dandelions.

The parkway verge was awash with horticultural bastards. And most cheerful they looked, too, swatches of butter-yellow against the tender green of young grass.

The dandelion cocks a snook at propriety and beams a sort of wicked grin back at creation. The dandelion is the floral equivalent of a short sharp blast on a kazoo. And there within sight of meticulously groomed, ever-so-proper, lovingly tended upper-crust yards and gardens, the little buggers were whooping it up. Cheered me enormously.

We can wallow in the Painfulness of Reality, and reality is in fact painful as hell at times—just as dandelions really are weeds. We can and should be ever aware of our status as very real Miserable Offenders. We do need to be careful and disciplined and honorable and integral and good in our daily lives. This is all true and important, because the alternative is chaos.

But.

Look at an average abandoned city lot and you'll find life upspringing, invading, taking over, breaking down the grim order we have created. Saplings spring up in the gutter of a roof, drawing nourishment from dead leaves. Weeds invade the pavement, breaking it up. Wild vines swarm and, with their fingers, reduce our work to rubble. Some people find this discouraging, because it says something about the transience of human works. I find it greatly cheering, because it speaks to me of life's abundance. It also appeals to my wicked side.

But it's more than that: it says to me that life doesn't have to be perfect to be glorious in its sheer aliveness. Love has nothing to do with perfection. After thinking about dandelions and how fond I am of the silly buggers, I begin to suspect that maybe God loves us *because* we are sinners, not in spite of that fact. I think of the people I love, and I know that I love them all the more for their humanity, not in spite of it. Knowing that a person is unsure and vulnerable and much less than perfect makes me love that person more, not less.

If human love is a reflection, however pale, of God's love for us, then maybe that says something about how God sees our faults and failings: not with blind-eyed indulgence, not minimizing the problems, but truly and with love. We are all such vulnerable children doing our best in a hard world. We are not perfect, weed-free lawns, and no matter how hard we work, we barely seem to stay ahead of the mess.

But we are loved, wholly and completely loved. And that's where the joy comes from, sneaking up on us, blooming like an upstart glowing dandelion, breaking through like daylight, lighting up the sun.

Subversives

On my walks this summer, I used to pass a strip where they'd dug up the roadside edges of people's lawns for municipal purposes. The strips had been filled in and smoothed over, but grass hadn't been sown, or hadn't taken, and the strips were alive with weeds.

Or that's what we call them. Adventurers, these plants, grabbing a blank spot when it opened, ready to seize the chance; nothing shy about them. Not demure conformist grass, not legally authorized flowers. Merely themselves.

Mostly what they had in common was a tough slenderness, a delicacy of leaf and flower. They were like those young, tough, fragile, pretty girls who you see on the corner, the ones who you know are aiming for trouble, but they're still breathtaking in their delicacy. The Methodist church at one point dutifully mowed its share of the weeds down, and I mourned the plants as they died in their flattened beauty on the sidewalk, but they came springing back: a tangle, intricate, lace-like, interleaving leaves, flowers (pale blue, pale yellow), and twining stems.

I don't know the names of half the plants I saw and admired, but I watched them succeed each other: the asters following the black-eyed Susans, while Queen Anne's lace folded its umbrils up into seed-making huddles that reminded me of a baby's gently clamped fist. And I thought: how do weeds fit into orthodoxy? Yes, I know, to grow the fields of corn and oats across the road from these ethereal vagrants, we are going to have to take protective measures. And some weeds are extremely aggressive and need tight control; purple loosestrife, for example. We can't afford weeds in our food supply. But food supply aside, I say, let the little buggers rip. They add to the fullness and complexity of things.

Who's defining what weeds are, and for what purposes? Isn't the perfect glassily-green suburban lawn a monument to man's itch to control and regulate God's creation? We spend an inordinate amount of time and effort (and do real environmental harm) trying to persuade plants to behave themselves as we want them to behave. Our clutchiness has nothing to do with the intrinsic beauty of the plants; the wild buckthorn scrub in the woods is as handsome a specimen as you'd find in any greenhouse—prettier than most weeping figs.

One thing about certain weeds—dandelions are one, plantain is another, camomile is a third—is that they invade the most barren terrain. Hereabouts, you'll find these three growing in the cracks in asphalt, along the edges of dirt or graveled roads, wherever other plants can't crowd or shade them out. They flourish under the most unpromising conditions.

Life has a way of invading, riotously, the spaces of life that we make dead. Joy has a way of upspringing, whether we think it's right or not. It sneaks up on us at inappropriate moments, like funerals or periods of intense pain, and we may try to squish it down again out of a sense that it Just Isn't Proper. "Life is real, life is earnest, and the grave is not its goal," as some God-awful Victorian once uttered.

Surely God delights in the vagrant, the unruly, the jokers—the weeds. Otherwise, they would lack this beauty. Which is considerable. Without them, my walk would lose much of its delight, its gentle wild streak. What, really, is the difference between a weed and a wildflower, but our convenience?

And I thought also: we need, all of us, to be tied to this earth, to have our toes in it—to be able to see ALL life, weeds included, and to see it honestly and lovingly, without having to reach for the hoe or the herbicide. For God made all, with love.

The Profligate

My maple trees are at it again.

There are three of them (there were four; I mourn the one we lost) and they are monumental, sturdy of trunk and ample of bough. These are *big* trees. They were probably planted when the house was built a century ago. They keep the sun off in summer, and the sound of their leaves is a continuous cool whisper. In winter they stand lace-like against the pale sky, breaking the violence of the winter wind. They are a comfort and a shelter and a refreshment for the eye and heart.

The bay window of my own room faces the westernmost tree, my personal favorite. Its presence, green or gold or wintry black, has been a constant in my life, while so much else has changed. I have lain in bed and seen that one diagonal branch across my window for nine full years. It has been there when I was full of light and happiness, and when I could hardly see it for tears.

Right now each of the three trees is a continuous slash of brilliance—one pure gold, one red-gold, one red-orange. And the leaves are in drifts. I'm struck, as I am each year, by the sheer abundance of life, the prodigality of God's creation. Each of my trees is dropping literally thousands of leaves, each leaf a miracle, composed of thousands of cells, capable of complex feats of biochemistry. Each leaf is as like, and unlike, its leaf-sibling as I am to you and you are to me. And these are only three out of thousands of maples in the township.

You can go a tiny bit off your rocker remembering that all this beauty, all this abundance, amounts to a pinprick within a small town within a province within a country on a small planet orbiting a third-rate star, while the Milky Way sweeps the sky with glory .

You can go daft just trying to wrap your mind around the generosity, the prodigiousness, the sheer exuberant *givingness* of God, who somehow manages to keep separate, known, and beloved each one of several billion individual human beings, yourself and myself included, not to mention maple trees. I can barely manage to love the handful of people he has given to me to love—and that not well.

Shivery thought. Time to go rake.

Big Grass

(With a special thanks to the Algonquin of Golden Lake, who are lending me the land that my house sits on until the Government of Canada gets around to paying them for it, sooner or later.)

I have just sat out on the back stoop and shucked a dozen ears of corn for my younger kid's birthday party. Remarkable stuff, corn. The clever people who held these Americas in trust from the Creator before we incomers took the ground out from under them are responsible for creating this plant, which they took very seriously indeed. They bred it from teosinte, a wild grass. Corn is in fact a giant grass, and the cobs in my hand are full of grass seed.

But these seeds will not sprout without human intervention. Corn cannot self-seed; without us, it would die out. The seed has no way of separating itself from the cob and fanning out to find fresh ground; if a cob fell and sprouted, the seedlings would choke each other out. Not, perhaps, a bad analogy for looking at how we stand in terms of God, with the signal difference that God has given us the ability to walk away from him—to choose, as the seeds of this very big grass cannot choose.

We start life with the firm belief that we are not created; we just are, and the universe is supposed to spin around us like a top 'round its axis. It takes a little while and a good many quite painful collisions with reality before we realize that we are not, in fact, at the center of the universe. Some of us, more strong-minded perhaps than the rest of us, never do manage to figure that out, and we all slide back into this state at times. But reality has a way of clonking us sharply upside the skull when we're being like this.

Once we've picked ourselves up for perhaps the eleventy-seventh time, nursing our bruises, we may finally discover a different aspect of reality: we are, in fact, weak and dependent and deeply imperfect creatures, truly Miserable Offenders. That discovery is apt to send us into spasms of anxiety and perfectionism or increasingly rigid denial. We try harder and harder to be good, to get it all together, to be everything we should be, to satisfy the rules; and as life presses in on us, we realize how very imperfectly we can do this. The Law can never be adequately lived up to. No matter how hard we try, we are failures, and our worst failure is often our inability to recognize that we must fail. We can never be worthy. Even as good Christians, we can never adequately balance the imperatives of the New Testament, and if we think we can, it's because we haven't looked at our consciences too closely. We wobble like a child in its mother's high heels and think that we're being so grown-up.

Once we fail often enough at being Good (an invaluable experience!), we begin to be aware that we aren't really in control of things—not even in control of ourselves, as we behave in ways we despise and cannot help. We are, quite truthfully, only living creatures: mortal, guilty. We may stick at that stage, locked in guilt and self-loathing, alternately falling back into the slough and trying to clamber out of it, or we may go looking for a god, something to fill the hole at the center. And if we have any sense, we will look not for any little god (like work or family or church or alcohol) but for The God. The Big God, the one all humankind always dimly senses.

But this God, the Big God, has the power to flatten us like cockroaches, and if we have two bits of spiritual common sense, we realize that that's exactly what we deserve—if nothing else, for our total inability to do an adequate job of loving ourselves, each other, or God. God's justice is truly to be feared, because none of us can possibly ever live up to God's laws. Not humanly possible, however hard we work at it.

Another fact about corn.

Agriculturally speaking, corn is a pain in the butt. It demands much fertilizer or two years' crop can wear out the soil for a decade. It needs a long growing season. It's a glutton for water. It needs careful crossbreeding. The ears now boiling, as the children chase each other around the house, had to be picked by hand, one ear at a time. It requires highly specialized machinery. It has serious pests. There are much, much more sensible crops to grow and eat.

So why do we grow it?

Because we love it.

So why doesn't God give us what we so richly deserve?

Because God loves us.

God loves us, not in a sweet-and-fluffy way, but with richness and poignancy and deep yearning for our very souls. My soul, your soul, the essence of who we are—that's what God wants, for our essential selves to pelt headlong into his open arms.

We were (and are) so sick of our own sin that we could not, cannot accept that love. We were (and are) so sick in our arrogance that we'd deny that love to others, condescending to them, insisting on standing between them and God's mercy and acceptance. Jesus told us of that love, and we responded with violent rejection. He upped the stakes; we adored and reviled him. He insisted; he put his life on the line to convince us. And God raised him and held him high, to prove Love to us.

It is the deepest and richest, warmest and most satisfying sort of paradox. We have to hold these two opposites in mind at once, not one at a time: we are indeed as grass, totally dependent, needy and demanding, fed on manure, incapable of growing on our own, and needing sometimes very tough treatment before life is done with us. And at the very same time—not alternately, but simultaneously—we are the graceful giants, prized, treasured, valued for our fruit, as beautiful in God's eyes as the corn was to those whose thoughtful breeding shaped it out of teosinte. We are both, and we are both at once.

Once we figure this out and learn to abide happily by paradox, instead of wanting to be simply good or simply sinful, we are free. We are free to grow to our full height, to produce the richness God laid down in the seed of our souls, to unfurl our talents and let them grow and bloom in the warmth and light of God's love. We can become as bold as this empress of grasses, firmly rooted but able to bend. And we can produce a hundredfold, a thousandfold, giving back to God what God wants from us most—ourselves, our souls and bodies, and the love that he calls us to become.

Blessed be God for corn. Among so very many other blessed creatures.

Milkweed

It is not, even at the height of summer, a particularly appealing plant, this milkweed. It is medium-sized, broad, and rather ungainly, with its large undistinguished, long-oval leaves, the sort of weed that really does look like a nuisance, as well as being one. And now that the first frosts have clipped its leaves off, it looks pathetic. The bare stalk rises, shriveled and ungainly, with its cluster of pods clutching to the top. The plant has gone from unwelcomed squat to dying gowk, with never a moment of real beauty.

The pods are less unlovely; broad at the bottom, they taper into a backward curve, like a comma. They were a quiet but rather pretty pale green; now they're turning to grey-green, then to mouse-brown with grey-green streaks. But again, these wouldn't be winners in any botanical beauty contest, not with their rough, scrubby pod-hides. It's only when the plant is dying and the pod splits that the miracle happens.

You pull the pod open and there they are, the seeds, rank upon rank of them by the dozen, neatly overlapping like a fish's scales. But no fish has scales of this beauty. Each seed is two-toned: pale mahogany at the center, then a delicate incised band with a frill, both in soft sienna brown. The mass of them lying close-lapped looks like a figure from a fine Oriental brocade or embroidery, complex, elegant, strong and delicate. The cone of seeds enfolds, and then rises into, the other half of the miracle: the thousands of superfine strands folded tightly together, cream-colored and polished to a high gloss. No silk has this sheen, this fineness. Fan the silk out and it is of such softness . . . and then you consider the miracle of its making; how the plant knows in its genome how to make such beauty, without even suspecting (in human terms) what it's up to—because ultimately, this beauty is there for purely practical reasons: to distribute the seeds.

When the frost and the wind are right, the pod unfolds and releases; the seeds cling for a moment to the lips of the pod and then are whirled into the air, from the dying stalk and the pod that withers and falls. So does the soul when the body releases it. Except, of course, that when our leaves are clipped and the stalk fails, and the pod shrivels and opens and the inner beauty unfolds—

when that happens, we aren't whisked randomly off in the wind but are brought to the Light and cupped most lovingly in the palm of our Creator's hand.

The Tying-Together Thing

A Mason jar filled with water and lilacs stands on the windowsill just to my left, and the scent of the flowers fills the room. When I was a girl, it was the custom in our (rather strict) high school that during lilac season, girls would bring branches of the flowers to class. For a week or so the scent of lilac would pierce the school-smell of floor wax and cleaning compound and young sweaty bodies, touched with the slightly sour gym-smell. I still remember my Parisian French teacher being startled half out of her wits when her students handed her a huge armload of lilac blossoms.

Later, when I was living miserably in the city, there would be touches of lilac—people from suburbia or the country bringing bunches in. Even in the toughly formal, coolly businesslike city core, I'd catch the odd whiff of that familiar scent and be, for a moment, in happier times and places. When I was in town yesterday, I brought in lilacs for my office, and so must other people have done. I saw a sleeping drunk propped up against a telephone pole, and someone had left a branch of lilac across his knees.

In the countryside, when they're in bloom and stand out by their color, you see the old racks of lilac. And you know there's a good chance that you're looking at what used to be somebody's home-place before the last child left and the parents died and the house burned down or fell into its own cellar. Alder and sumac have moved in over the unused fields, which should never have been farmed at all, except that humanity is forever hopeful. But the lilacs are still there, and apple trees, gone back to their wild toughness, both doing just fine on their own and very much at home in the wild.

Lilacs tie my life together; their scent crosses the chasms between the sections of my life. It is a constant throughout the sharp discontinuities, the lost times and found times, the periods of pain and peace.

The word "religion" comes from the same root as "ligament" and means "tying together." When I sing the *Sursum corda* each Sunday in church, I am singing words that go back in time almost to our earliest roots and which reach around the world. These words tie me to monks at Glastonbury in the twelfth century and to Ugandan women today. They tie me to Latin-speaking Christians in ancient Rome and to Inuktituk-speaking Inuit of the High Arctic. My family, people I love and have never seen, people I love and have lost, will have said or sung these same words this same Sunday morning. These words, like lilac, tie my life together. Tie our lives together. Tie us in the community of saints and sinners (which we are, all of us) over time and space. Tie us to God's Son's life among us. Tie us to God godself.

And like lilac, religion is remarkably hard to get rid of. Just try repressing a lilac. Prune it, and it will spring up again stronger than ever. Let it age, and as it grows older, its roots will tunnel under the earth and, finding promising ground, send up a dozen, a hundred suckers, each an infant lilac bush. Even as the central shrub grows old and begins to die back—lilacs too are mortal, after all—the new growth sets its roots stronger and deeper, and reaches up for sun, and grows in strength, and starts to bloom.

Hope and memory, unity and community, apparent fragility and real toughness, a vulnerable sweetness, a freshness even in the grey center of the city, something rare and commonplace, coming back time and time and time again, no matter what Real Life does to repress and ignore it. Faith and lilacs.

An afterthought:

After reading this, someone wrote back: "I too have a special place in my heart for lilacs. But tinged with my joy at their presence always comes a sorrow that their season is so short. It feels like I barely have time to savor their beauty and their scent before they're passed on."

But that might be an important part of their significance. Lilacs, unlike roses and carnations and even freesias (which I also love) can't be forced. You can only "do" lilacs for about a week to ten days each year. This stubborn seasonality is, I think, important. We get used to having asparagus in January, even if it's overpriced and not very good.

Some things, thank God, can't be put off until we have the leisure to get around to them; some things have to be savored lovingly, in season, while they're there, because they won't await our convenience. Lilacs are one such; babies are another; love is a third. Some things just can't survive being put on indefinite hold, until we've got the time to spare for them from More Important Matters.

Has something to do with living life with one foot in this world and one in the next. The foot in this world must, I think, be grounded honestly and properly in this world—which means living with seasonality and loss and change and the like, instead of pretending that the lilacs will be there later, or the kid can wait, or (s)he'll still be there when I've got this project finished. Has to do with what we choose to love and what we choose to see as secondary—what we care for, and what we're prepared to give.

-2-

Staring at the Cat Bowl

Max

Max-cat sits serenely by his food dish. No great anxiety crosses his handsome grey-tabby face; he knows that sooner or later, I'll notice that the dish could use a little topping up. Not that it's empty; if it were, Max would be telling me in no uncertain terms. It's just not quite as full of kibble as it could be. Max is a patient cat, with lovely manners. He sits, he waits.

None of my three personal representatives of the order Felidae can, of course, see me as a person with other responsibilities, another life. I am there for *them*. Nobody ever claimed that cats were selfless or other-centered. I'm not their owner, because cats don't "do" ownership/owned relationships. We share a space. I provide the kibble and love and attention; they provide amusement value (the sight of a cat killing a pair of rolled-up socks with professional thoroughness can have me in stitches) and companionship, and they are a reminder of Nature at her most natural.

They have their individual personalities, their individual beauty: stolid, comfortable, dignified, undemanding grey-tabby Max, the Beach Ball That Walked Like a Cat; Jenny Jemima, the tortoise-shell with a coat of pure silk, an ugly-pug little face, and very sweet manners; Dynamite, gloss-black with sad yellow eyes, who is still skittish after being abandoned, who jumps at the slightest noise, but who can curl up trustingly when I hold him and who purrs ecstatically when he's relaxed and I'm scratching his hard little belly.

It has been observed by my favorite theologian that we tend to regard God in much the same way that domestic cats regard their personal human beings: there when they need us to fuss them or top up the food dish, there, freezing our toes off, holding the door open while they ponder the Out and In options (Jenny-cat likes to study these very carefully and at great length).

Max, sitting patiently and waiting for a scoop of kibble, reminds me of our own attitude toward prayer. We may have lovely manners, asking God to provide for us in whatever way seems best to him without screaming or nagging about our own needs, but the fact is that we're sitting here waiting for him to top up the kibble. It is inconceivable to us that God might be busy filling up someone else's need and might want us to consider the possibility that there is, after all, still some food in the dish. This is because there isn't one of us who isn't, at some level, me-centered. That's part of human nature.

Cats are serenely selfish and it doesn't bother them in the least, because they're cats. That is how God intended them to be. They have no calling to be otherwise. There is no sin in their being totally centered on their own needs and comfort, because they're cats. If a cat manages to rise above its nature and be a genuinely loving being—and some cats, I think, do manage this—then that's frosting on the cake. If a cat is not loving, it has not missed its mark as a being.

But we aren't cats, even if we'd like to be like them—as unworried, as self-centered, as happily materialistic as they are, as untroubled as they are by any notion that we should be otherwise. Fortunately or un-, we aren't cats; we're human. We're called upon to be totally un-catlike in becoming loving, giving, deeply aware of ourselves and others, growing (sometimes quite painfully) toward a fullness of life and soul that isn't in the feline deck of cards, or if it is, it's in ways that we don't know about. We can, of course, try to be cats instead of people, but ultimately that won't work very well, because ultimately we get to answer to God for what we've made of the souls God endowed us with. And if God had meant us to be cats, we'd be cats.

Don't get me wrong, I love my cats. They cannot love me, because they can't even see me except as She-Who-Fills-Our-Cat-Bowl and a familiar physical presence and smell, but that's fine. I know that's just the way things are, and I don't expect recognition or love from them. Merely, I know that I'm not a cat and they aren't human beings. I am a human being and not God, and God is God and not a human being. Or a cat, for that matter.

In the Shell

The man at the reptile exhibit at the mall was explaining turtle shells to a knot of ten-year-olds. "People think that the turtle's shell is separate and the turtle can come out," he said, handling a large painted turtle with pride and love and gentleness, showing off its beauty. "But the shell's not separate." He traced lines with one finger on the handsome carapace, telling the kids how the shell is fused with the turtle's rib cage and is part of the animal, not an outward thing at all. "If you tried to take the turtle out of its shell, it'd kill the turtle," he said.

That's not how we normally think of turtles. We think of the turtle as being in its shell the way we are in our clothes—separate from it, able to take the thing off. But, in fact, when we think we're thinking about turtles, maybe we're really thinking about us. Maybe we're thinking about our own tendency to want to be guarded, to front the world with a tough, protective shell. Maybe we're thinking about how we want to keep our vulnerable selves well covered and safe. Not surprising, given how this world works . . .

When we first ate of the fruit of the knowledge of good and evil, we set the good apart in one place, separating it out, and in so doing we created evil. We're subjected to evil throughout our journey: from the bully on the school playground, from those who turn away in fear and selfishness when we need them, from callousness and rejection in the work world, from disappointment and betrayal in love, from loss and grief and injuries of all sorts. We learn before we're even full grown that we can't afford to be vulnerable to the world. Not unless we want to be pounded into applesauce.

Worse still, we're told that gentleness is weakness, that love is just asking for grief, that generosity is fecklessness, that openness is cruisin' for a bruisin'. We're told that it's right to be smart, strong, tough, guarded, and independent. That's being grown-up; anything else is stupid kid stuff. Anything else is just asking for trouble. Anything else is holding out your heart to be drop-kicked across the room.

We learn to wear our tough and handsome carapace and to keep our vulnerabilities inward, because those are this world's rules. In times of danger we learn to tuck head and extremities in, hunkering down, playing it super-safe. Being cool. Being contained. Not showing that it hurts or that we care or that it really does matter a whole lot.

But if that's how we're supposed to be, why is this shell so heavy? Why does it cost us so much to drag it around? And why is the safe darkness inside it so ultimately unsatisfying? so lonely? so hollow-feeling? such a sorry place to live?

Turtles may be constructed by God and natural selection to wear their ribs fused to their outside shells, but we weren't intended to be that way. We were intended to be in love and communion with others, to be free, to be open, to trust, to love and be loved. No baby comes into this world stoical and self-contained, wishing to be separate and strong. That lesson is one we learn the very hard way, because it goes against God's desire for us.

If we have the sense God gave a goose, we will find places in our lives where we can take our shells off. We'll look for and find people with whom we can be trusting and unguarded, gentle and open and loving. We'll find opportunities for the exchange of genuine love, and if people fail us, we'll know somehow that we're supposed to go on looking. Not because we're fools, but because we're responding to what God wants us to be and to become. We're drawn to this change because we're being called toward health and wholeness and becoming the selves that God intends us to be.

It takes courage to slip out of that shell and stand shivering for the first time, naked and frightened and deeply ashamed of how we really look. The first touch of air may fall chill on our unaccustomed flesh. But as the Son of God's light and love and healing touch our thin, pale skins, we're warmed and strengthened. We gain color and cheerfulness and a gentle toughness—a true, good hide grown from confidence and love, not a shell grown from fearfulness and rigid defensiveness. And we find that perhaps the shell isn't so very necessary all the time. Maybe not even most of the time. Maybe only a little of the time . . . Maybe not at all.

Another Twilight

Was out last evening tending to the barbecue just at that time of dusk when the light slips away and you lose your color vision. Even as I watched, turning the food on the grill, I lost the green of grass and leaves, and the world turned first to an oddly khaki color, then to shades of pure grey. There was still light enough to see, but the familiar outlines were made strange, as though filtered through a different atmosphere. A sort of reality shift, like looking through water.

I saw a bat swooping after mosquitos. I saw fireflies. Moths circled and smacked on the light by the back door. I became aware of my cats prowling the yard with deft professionalism—no longer the familiar furry individuals I share my house with but territorial predators doing their job, doing it well, with priorities I can only guess at.

This world of half-light is *their* world; I am only a visitor in it, tolerated as familiar She-Who-Fills-the-Cat-Bowl. Unlike them, I am incapable of moving with this swift confidence in a landscape I can't fully see. Jenny-cat came up, reassured me with a quick brush of silky fur against my leg, and then sprang lithely off, completely confident and comfortable, into a deepening gloom where she is entirely at home and I can't set my clumsy human feet with any safety.

This was another world, a foreignness superimposed on the same grass and stone wall and picnic table and shrubs and trees that, at noon, were bright and familiar and full of normalcy and light. And Lord only knows what other world the bat saw (or rather heard), and the fireflies and moths . . . what realities do they know that I'm utterly unaware of, as I'm unaware of the smell-world that my cats and the next-door dog know so intimately?

Fish presumably aren't aware of the world of air because they live wholly in the water; moths presumably are equally unaware of the world of water. Whales presumably are aware of both worlds, because they dwell in both. Bats are aware of an echo-world that whales know something about, but I don't, and nor do my cats. My cats inhabit a world of sounds and scents that they share with dogs (but presumably not with trees?). And God alone knows what the trees are sensing. What does the milkweed sense that turns this gene off and that one on?

There is a whole world under the bent leaf of the grass, and I haven't got a clue what's going on in it. There is a microcivilization alive in the intricate world of yard garbage—pruned wood and leaf-litter—back behind the wall. Within its sprawling tangle of decaying branches and wild grape, creatures move and live, copulate, birth and rear their young, fall sick and die and decay. I can't even begin to imagine what their world looks like to them.

What we pick up with our five blunt senses and process with our arrogant intelligence is, in some ways, so much, and so very little. Our senses take out of this world only what they are equipped to take up, and they are sieves, not scoops. We can perceive a certain range of light waves, certain frequencies of sound, certain smells and flavors, certain stimuli, but not *all* light waves or frequencies or smells and flavors or stimuli. We know one range of the world's beauty. My cats, hunting at dusk, know another.

But there's another kind of sensing, not of the eyes or ears or nose or tongue or skin, but a sensing of the spirit. Humans of all cultures, all eras, are aware of a Something other than the daylight life of this world. It may scare them; they may reject it, deny their awareness, deafen themselves to its whisper. Or more universally, they grasp at their awareness in myth and magic, religion and ceremony. They wash themselves in the fragrance of the censer, in the sweetgrass smudge, in the wavering thread of smoke from a stick of incense, in the sprinkled fragrant oils. They purify themselves in ways that have much, and little, to do with taking a bath. They break bread in a meal which is parallel to the reality of the food I turned on the barbecue but which is taken and eaten at a wholly different level. They sense a reality superimposed on this world but not entirely of it. A world of meaning, of soulfulness, of life lived just beyond the periphery of our daylight vision. "Over my head, I hear music in the air," the spiritual sings. "There must be a God somewhere."

-3-

"Shall We Gather at the River"

Darker Colors

The weather has finally broken. We still haven't had enough rain—we need about three days' solid soaking to make up for a month of baking drought. But today the sky was cool grey and the temperature was almost chilly.

Out for a walk this evening, I noticed what always surprises me: at least here in Ontario, nature is more intensely colored under a grey sky than under a sunny one. It's as though sunlight bleaches things out. The leaf greens tonight were rich and sensual compared with the dusty, weary olive tone they take on under blasting sunlight. I noted also that a border of weeds had a delicacy of line and color, a lace-like intricacy and beauty, that elude my neighbors' carefully tended flowerbeds.

I've noticed this in fall, too, when the leaves are turning. In wet weather the colors take on a depth and richness of tone; the blacks are blacker, the golds deeper, the reds more solemn and splendid. It's as though the loss of direct bright light seems to bring out an intensity.

I've noticed something of the same effect in people. It seems to me that the people I know who have (as a friend once put it) "done forty laps in the desert" have something of a greater richness, a deeper color, than those who have had it comparatively easy. But then again, I discover as I grow older that very few people have had it comparatively easy, and most souls have their own depth and richness, although the colors are not my own and may seem strange to me.

There are bright gifts and dark gifts, and we're as enriched by the dark gifts as by the bright ones. We are the more fully colored for being somewhat shadowed. The more we learn to see and accept that shadowy quality, which is really the quality of being truly human and therefore vulnerable and imperfect, paradoxically the richer we become.

The sky just dimmed, and the rain has begun to descend in fat silver sheets, coming in waves that roar on the porch roof, bringing a sudden refreshing chill. I think I'll go stand on the front porch and watch it rain for a while.

Not a Gas

As I opened the back door to let Max-cat out a few minutes ago, a spume of snow swirling around the corner of the house caught me in the face. As I waited for Max to consider his in/out options, which takes a while, I could hear something I haven't heard in months: the sound of the creek at the bottom of my field.

I'd noticed, crossing the upstream bridge on a walk earlier today, that the thaw is truly on. The creek is swollen, churning, choked with green ice, breaking out irresistibly. Trees stand forlornly in its midst as it floods. It's sweeping out, finding its level, bursting forth, wild and fresh, and you'd better not argue with it for the next few weeks. For water will have its own way, regardless.

Miraculous stuff, water.

For starters, it shouldn't be a liquid. Its molecules are too small, the same size, roughly, as those of methane gas. What holds it together are the gazillions of tiny impermanent bonds tugging one molecule close to the next. If the oxygen atom is firmly tied by formal chemical bonds to its two hydrogens, it's also flirting madly with the hydrogen next door, and its personal hydrogens are being gently but impermanently seduced by neighborhood oxygens. These transient bonds are enough to keep the whole mass glued together.

Next, while water does have its areas of internal order, these are (if I remember) somewhat random and chaotic and transient. Loosey-goosey stuff, water, of an independent nature, disliking being organized except locally, resisting compression, finding its own level, and you're best not to try to tell it otherwise. Water does what its nature tells it to do. Unless, of course, you chill the stuff down far enough, at which point it becomes formal, static, quite beautiful, and, on the whole, largely immobile ice.

Third, molecules are bouncing off the water into the air and diving back into the water in equilibrium, unless you heat the stuff up, at which point it gets extremely agitated and more and more molecules bounce out of the whole and go flying off into space. Molecules escape the bonds in ice, too, subliming into vapor. The three forms are always in equilibrium, although what that equilibrium is may depend on things like the temperature.

Fourth, of course, without water I would not be typing at my computer. And you would not be reading what I am writing. And Max-cat would not be checking out the backyard fauna, which would also not exist. Water inhabits the air and land and all things live, and most things unliving as well, and our Lord and Savior was substantially composed of it, just like us; and our water is as salty as the sea.

Fifth, water is marvelously expressive stuff, full of deep meaning to all humankind, perhaps the most beautifully symbolic stuff of all. The water of life, the water of baptism, the water that cleanses and heals, the water that breaks down and destroys, the water that lifts us and floats us when we come aground, the water that churns and pounds us out of our complacency and into awareness; the water of swamps and sloughs and soggy despond; the roiling sea-ice powerfully sculpting a coast; soft groundwater, tenderly upwelling to green a barren landscape; the singing chuckle of a creek, the roar of a fall, the calm assurance of a great river, the crash of a sea swell, the quiet privacy of fog, rain washing or slashing or downpouring or falling gentle as a leaf; the soft healing, or bitter springing, or joyful welling of salt tears.

This water I hear tonight will tumble from one river to the next, handed over from the creek to the Rideau to the Ottawa, from the Ottawa to the great St. Lawrence at Lac des Deux Montagnes, and then down past Quebec and out into the Gulf, sweeping past Baie Verte and my lost cove, until it reaches the open sea. It surrounds and suffuses us and is about our paths and our ways, and we aren't even conscious of it most of the time, except when we have too much or too little. Rather like the Holy Spirit, I suspect.

God be praised for the gift of water.

The Plumber

Last year the pipe from the well to the house gave up the ghost. It was galvanized piping, and we have extremely hard water; over the years the crud had built up, giving the supply pipe the plumbing equivalent of hardening of the arteries. Finally the thing died.

Art Munro, my faithful plumber (God reserves a place next to his throne for plumbers like this, right next to whoever invented lox on a bagel with cream cheese) studied the situation and, drawing on his vast experience and getting a little creative, he devised a scheme. For several hours thereafter, the house jangled and thumped and rang as Art and his son and their large-but-not-too-swift assistants, using sledge hammers, systematically pounded a piece of two-inch pipe underground from my house to the well, drilling a hole for the new supply pipe to go through. It says something that Art hit the well bang on and the whole thing worked like a charm. And if the pipe ever needs to be replaced again, the job will be easy.

While they were hammering the pipe through, I made coffee and took it down to the basement and tried to make small talk, which is not easy when a large young man is pounding a length of pipe with a sledgehammer in a relatively confined space . . . until I realized that they really didn't want me there. No offense, ma'am, and nothing against you personally. They were busy; they had a job to do. And so I went back upstairs and got on with whatever needed to be done.

It was sometime later that I realized that there are times when God does the same thing. More quietly, though. God, being God, seems not to need to hammer pipes through the underground with a sledgehammer—or maybe God has not seen fit to do this to me. At least not yet. You never know, though. God, being creative, uses whatever tactics will work, and sometimes the tactics can be a little startling.

If you're into this religion business, you spend a lot of time listening for the Small Voice in your head, the one that whispers "Yes" or "No" or just "I love you." But there are times when the Voice is not there, and those are terribly discouraging times. There are times when you really do feel lost and alone. These are what the religious literature refers to as the Dark Night of the Soul or the Slough of Despond. They are not the same as just being unhappy or depressed; they are different. These are times when you have to take faith on faith and wait, dry-souled and patient. It's only long afterward that you can see how productive these times, in fact, have been.

I was mired in one of those dry spells not long after the well-pipe incident when . . . okay, please don't see this as certifiable behavior . . . I swear I heard, in the silent corner of my mind where the Voice is usually to be found, a very small *clank*. A *clank* as of a handtool being dropped on a hard surface. I could have sworn I heard a muffled curse as well.

Don't take that too literally.

The Creek

Finally, *finally*, FINALLY, it's spring.

This has been the slowest, stubbornest, sullenest spring I can remember here—a long, spaced-out, dreary time between last snow and first green. And even now spring is moving verrrry slowly. My three huge maple trees are still only at bud stage, and the lilacs are well behindhand. But the grass is brilliantly alive, the scrub woods have a mist of soft green on them, and down at the bottom of my field the creek is sparkling.

It was in March nine years ago that I went back to church after being away for almost twenty years. I went back for my kids. I wanted them to have something I had grown up with: their mother's heritage. Of course, I couldn't give them exactly what I'd had—different times, different places. But I could give them something of what I'd had. I had no thought for what the process might do to me. Talk about the original bait-and-switch operation!

It was, I remember, at about this stage of that spring, after I'd been back a couple of months, that the fear hit. It was quite serious fear too. I visualized myself standing in the dry bed of a river, among a mass of tumbled pale rocks worn smooth by water but now entirely dry. Dry as a withered chili. Not so much as a drop of damp in sight. But I felt, could hear, a deep rumble, as of something mighty in motion, far off, but not far *enough* off.

I remember thinking: God's love is going to be a flash flood. I am going to be swept away. I, me, the person I am—I will be caught up and tumbled end over end and carried downstream like an ant down the bathtub drain. I found this image terrifying. If *real* faith, *real* God, *real* love caught up with me, whatever was going to become of *me*?

So I prayed, treasonably and selfishly and in complete cowardice of spirit: Please, God, not a torrent. I don't think I can handle a torrent. Give me a trickle. Just a trickle. I'm pretty sure I can handle that much.

What's that old line? Be careful what you pray for—you may get what you ask for. What I got in the way of faith was a trickle. Only a trickle. My devotions are pathetic. Sometimes I manage a bit of concentrated prayer. Sometimes I manage a bit of Bible reading. I do get to church most weeks. I do listen to some religious music. I write. I spend a lot of time hanging around my cyberparish. But real discipline, formal prayer, contemplation, confession, intercession, formal theology—I can't seem to manage those very well. My mind slides off sideways like a car on a glass-ice road, ever so gently drifting ditchward. I'm too easily distracted, I guess.

Similarly, my faith is not exactly mighty. It's risen with the years until it's a not-so-tiny creek, like the creek down at the back; but it never rises as high as the creek does in spring, nor does it fall as far as the creek does in late summer, for that matter. Definitely in the mustard-seed division, my faith. Doesn't seem to be growing a whole lot either.

But the land along-shore the creek of my belief . . . now that's another matter. That land, which had been sere and brown and dry as dust, a famished land full of little more than desolation, seems to be getting very green, as though the groundwater has been quietly seeping upward from below. And the green is spreading, blooming, bringing to new life so much of what had before been killed off by early frosts, softening so much that had been baked to hardness by long drought.

As spring comes slowly back to this mud-brown land after such a long winter, it comes back first in the grass underfoot, almost unnoticeably. Then it seems to spread upward and outward. Just so does grace operate: first under our feet, where we can't even see it, and then, when we begin to see and accept it, higher and deeper and farther and wider than we can even begin to ask or imagine.

And all I did was to say "yes." Not a big, happy "yes" either but a small, conditional, half-hearted, deeply fearful "yes." The least unclenching of the fist of my heart, the least softening of my tough, suspicious, resistant hide, and there it was: the opening God had so desperately wanted all along.

It was a poor excuse for a "yes" I managed, those nine years ago, and I couldn't have done it at all except for my kids (Love, being sneaky, tends to make the most of love); but it was a "yes" nonetheless. I'll take a little water, Lord. A little love. Not too much, not more than I'm ready for. I know I can't drink, so just let me sip. It may not be as much as you want to give me, perhaps, and I'm sorry my capacity is so very limited compared with your grace. But yes, I think I will take a little, please. Thank you.

If we don't dig our heels in, Love goes before, nudging us gently, almost imperceptibly, into position, until we find ourselves in a place where that "yes" becomes possible. And then God gives us what God knows we need and are ready and able to accept. No more, no less. All God asks us to do is to swallow our pridefulness and fear, and to say "yes" just a little, however slowly, stubbornly, sullenly we speak the word. But it gets easier with practice.

Yes, yes—the answer of course is yes.

Part 2

One Foot in the Furrow

-4-

Three Landscapes

Beachwalking

I spent a month this past summer on Baie Verte, a sliver of calm, warm water wedged between Nova Scotia and New Brunswick, and most evenings, tide permitting, I got out on the flats at low tide for a walk.

The land is low in this place, flowing into saltwater marshes that the Acadians diked and farmed. The soil is thick, red clay with patches of deep-red sandstone. It is calm and lonely country. It's hard to imagine, during late summer, when the land looks domesticated, exactly how bleak and ferocious and cold it can be here in winter, when the great storms rip across the shelterless salt marshes with no mercy whatsoever and the sea tears another few hundred tons of earth from the shore, toppling the edging trees and flinging great boulders around like marbles.

But in summer there's no gentler place I know. The cove where I love to walk is broad and extremely shallow; at low tide you can walk almost a half mile out on flats and sandbars before you come to water, and you can wade another hundred yards before the water gets much past your knees. The light is diffuse, the air is mild and fresh, and the flats are the soft, rosy color of brick. The silver saltwater around my ankles, when I take to wading, is warm with the sun's warmth on the flats, and the weeds tickle tentatively as the crabs scuttle for safety.

Beachwalking is a good time to cleanse the soul; you can trace a sin on a stone and throw it humming through the air, to be washed clean by the healing saltwater. Wonderful stuff for rinsing wounds, saltwater is. You can walk from one pinkish sandbar to the next, splashing through the shallows and feeling the weight of the world slide off your shoulders.

Or you can watch the tide. You can meditate on how, twice each day, in a dance that moves around the clock, the soft silver-green water advances up over the flats, cleaning them, restoring them, refreshing them. You can stand at the tide's edge and watch the water come in a quarter-inch at a time, pushing a lace edge of foam before it. Each inch-long stretch of the tide's leading edge is what chaos theory calls a fractal, a pattern that seems random and can't be described by simple geometry but is in fact symmetrical, perfect, endlessly repeated. The water moves so gently, almost diffidently, advancing and retreating, moving over the sand softly, a little at a time. And yet, there are the tumbled boulders, the toppled trees. Such latent power the water has.

What's astonishing about tidal flats is their hidden life. From a distance you see only clean, plain, pale-red bars standing between the stripes of silver water, patches of eelgrass lying like shadows. You have to be out on the flats to become aware of the sheer volume of life they hold—literally thousands of clams, for example, in our one small cove; the crows and herons and gulls all searching for food; the plovers skimming like team aerobats; the waterbugs, the winkles, the worms, the mollusks, the nameless things dwelling in soft muck.

This land is deceptive that way—until the wind shifts ever so slightly and the incoming tide peacefully lays a couple of tons of spongy weed on the beach, just to remind you . . . And then you think that this is a small cove off a small bay off a strait off an ocean, and there are thousands and thousands of miles of this life, just in Nova Scotia. Mind-boggling, it is.

God, too, may be hidden, secreted, in life. We are aware, more or less, of God's action in our lives, but I doubt if too many people have any idea of exactly *how* busy God gets. We may be aware of the Big Stuff that God does with/for/to/on/in us, but I'm always uneasily aware that there's probably an awful lot of Providence going on in my daily life, in the lives of God-knows-how-many human souls—in plovers' lives and razor clams' lives even—that I am simply not aware of, nor paying proper attention to.

We brace ourselves for rough handling, expecting (perhaps) God to come down on us the way the sea descends on that shore in winter, tearing up the scenery, wrestling and brawling, throwing things around, radically reshaping our lives, playing rough. We expect to be tumbled end over end by religious experience. And for some, that is indeed what happens.

But God may act in infinitely small ways, so gently, so imperceptibly, that it's not until long afterward, when we look back and see the landscape so radically transformed by the gentlest of means, that we understand a great truth: our Lord is indeed a sneaky #@*!%.

I think I will take this new mystery away and chew on it for a while. This, to me, is harder to get my head around than (even) the glory of the galaxies and space immeasurable. God is around, in, through, over, beside, above, below each one of us, all however-many-billion human souls we are, not to mention winkles: drawing us ever closer to his immeasurable love in ways that we cannot begin to imagine.

Nothing Special

This is not beautiful country.

It's not ugly either. Among other places, I've lived in Vermont, where the landscape is gravely beautiful, and in Nova Scotia, which can be extraordinarily uncompromising. This landscape is simply undistinguished, like the plump, pudding-faced matron whom you'd never remember from one supermarket sighting to the next.

To the east is the flat, rich alluvial farmland left by the Laurentian Sea—strange country. To the west is the Canadian Shield, which manages to be both grim *and* beautiful—as Scottish as its settlers. My countryside is on the cusp between them. It's marginal farmland, much of it heading back into scrub deciduous forest or cedar bog, although it grows good apples. It rolls just enough not to be flat. It rises to real prettiness in early summer, when it is very green, and in some lights in winter, when it takes on a mystically blue whiteness. The rest of the time it's just . . . there. Plain-ish. Undistinguished. There is nothing special about it. It has no dignity or beauty to make you take notice of it. There is nothing attractive about it, nothing that would draw you to it.

When I first moved to this neck of the woods twenty-five years ago this summer, it was to the city; and it was a very dark time in my life. Being an immigrant and young and poor and unvalued and lonely and very frightened was no fun. Standing on a downtown bridge that I crossed every day on my way to work, I could look across the river to the Gatineaus in Quebec, low green hills that reminded me of home, where the mountains had always made me feel sheltered and comforted. I yearned for those hills with such an intensity of longing that I thought I would die. But I had no way of getting there.

But that was long ago, and I long since gave up on ever getting back into mountains. Now I'm forty minutes from the city, on the fringe of a small town, and after nine years here, I think I'm coming to be very fond of this country.

If you're willing to overlook the absence of Significant Scenery, you start noticing the racks of wild lilac. Or the gentle curve of a bump of land across the creek. Or the way an abandoned barn stands against a sky of soft cyan blue. If you're willing to accept the absence of mature and handsome forest, you can see an intricate loveliness in the soft grey-brown depths of the cedar bog. Or you might come up a lane through arching woods, opening into the crabbed beauty of an apple orchard, with a small plain limestone house standing like a serious child at the head of the low, fruit-laden trees.

Of course, God *could* choose to see that we have no dignity or beauty to make God take notice of us—or nowhere near enough anyway. God *could* choose to see that there is nothing attractive about us, nothing that would draw God to us. God could choose to despise and reject us, or, more likely, just not to be very interested in us. After all, that's what we've done to God's Son. "No one would even look at him—we ignored him as if he were nothing" (Isaiah 53:2-3).

Instead, into our lives, as into this landscape at the beginning of a very late spring, there comes a greenness, a growth, slow at first and with setbacks and cold and rainy days, but still . . . And this is because God (if we're willing to give God even a toe in the door) chooses instead to see beauty and dignity and attraction in us, the souls of God's own creating. God chooses to love us. We choose to accept that love or to turn away from it. Our decision, and God respects our privacy.

One corner of me will always long for the mountains of my home country, just as one corner of me longs for the Home across the River. Whenever I cross back into my own country, feel the swell of the mountains and the familiar curve of the roads, smell the clean, damp scent of those woods again, then I know I'm truly home.

But increasingly I find myself content in *this* soil, *this* life, willing to take whatever beauty's on offer wherever I can find it, willing to look with an accepting eye. I have, almost against my will, chosen to love this place, at least a little, to see it as beautiful in its quieter way. Responding to the little love I spare for it, it gives up its small beauties to me, confiding them to me, like the scent of wild lilac. If a landscape can have a soul, this land's soul has a gentle modesty about it, a quietness, a kindness, a soft diffidence I find pleasing.

Maybe this landscape has something to teach me, if I'm willing to learn. Maybe it teaches me the limits of my ability to love. For I know in my heart that this country is as lovely in God's eyes as are the mountains I still long for after all these years. It's my human, fallible, skew-whiffy vision that misses so much that God sees and knows and loves, whether in countrysides or in the human heart.

Kingdom Come

To get there, you have to clamber. From the east (which is how I first approached it), you climb sharply up from the pretty county town, then more slowly up the river valley, the road twisting and turning between the deep flanks of mountains calm as cattle. At the village you turn and climb more steeply still, along a narrower road, even more convoluted, past fewer houses as the land folds sharply upward and the hills squeeze tighter together. At the town line, the woods close in, arching above you. The forest floor is veiled with ferns, and their scent enters you like unsung music. You begin to hear the brook, which now runs close to the road, the sound of water so cold and pure it makes you ache.

There is more scenic country than this. Here, the ridges are too close-packed, too dense for vistas of the breath-stopping sort, the ones that let you see the mountains properly, ranged in their great strength and age and power. Here there are only compact dells and deep-folded valleys and sudden swooping hayfields taking off wherever the slope of the land permits, which is not often.

People had tried to farm here, two centuries since, and many of their great, grave, handsome houses survive, but the farms themselves gave up the struggle long ago. Their old stone walls run through the woods, and the cellar holes of fallen-in farm-steads are pocket swamps for the unwary. The country survived this senseless intrusion, and when these foolhardy intruders left off disturbing it in ways that did not suit it, it went back to doing what it does best: growing trees. And there lies its beauty.

For while there is more scenic country, country more to the popular taste, very little country could be more beautiful than this. Its beauty is not the sort that photographs well in the travel magazines. If that sort of beauty is the beauty of a young girl, this is the beauty of a woman with years and wisdom on her skin. This country has a quality that runs deeper, stranger, more compelling, and far richer. The green is curiously intense yet peaceful, like a child's clear, calm, intent gaze.

When you look into these woods, something tugs your vision in gently, pulling you deeper and deeper into the further reaches, toward a great something that lies at the heart of things. You want to walk into the woods and keep walking until you find their heart, over the next hill, in the next valley. The very air seems as satisfying as wine; the icy spring water slakes a thirst you didn't know you owned.

After you've stared at these woods long enough, after you have let them take possession of you, enfold you, smooth you out, take gentle hold of your being, something very odd happens. All those things that other people seem to care about so much—manicured lawns, vacation packages, correctly fashionable clothing, decorator placemats, retirement savings plans—don't really seem so terribly important to you. You can see that they're nice enough in their way, but you can't see what the fuss is about. You find that all those things that you thought you admired greatly—intellectual achievement, professional ability, the strive of individuality—are still good, as far as they go, but not sufficiently good; there's something missing there. They are oddly flat. The pleasures that you thought would fill your soul are indeed lovely, but ultimately they only leave it aching for this something else, whatever it was, that you sensed in the heart of this country.

And you know that you will not find the true fullness of that something on this side of the River; it waits for you on the far shore. You know also that you could not, in this life and with these senses, begin to taste or see or smell or hear or feel it; it is too large, too strong for you now. This richness, so palely reflected in what you see in the woods, if you could grasp its reality, would kill you as dead as one of these great, grey lichened boulders.

But you also know, with all your soul and being, that you'll know that something when you find it, because you smelled it, sensed it, felt its core in your core, in this piece of the kingdom on Earth.

-5-

Come Wind, Come Weather

Another Country

I was out for my usual walk on Wednesday evening, just about sunset. I was crisscrossing a field on a shortcut, a difficult path. Heavy vehicles had dug deep ruts, which had baked dry and hardened—the sort of path where you really do have to watch where you put your feet. Also, my mind was full of a problem as deeply rutted and hard-baked as the path. So I kept my eyes on my feet and my mind on my problem.

Something made me look up. Do you know that fading-out-blue that the sky turns sometimes, just at dawn or dusk? Cyan-blue but fading almost to silver. Thin, swirling strata of clouds swept across the sky, dark and light, a complex pattern. If you used a little imagination, you could see a shoreline in the sky. Another country, beautiful and almost within reach.

And then I thought: there is eternity. There, on the other side, on that shore, where we no longer see through a faded mirror, but directly—there is the life that this life is a preparation for. In that life this rutted path (both of body and of mind) will be so understandable, so thoroughly resolved. I will see, I will understand, I will know.

For a moment time itself dissolved and I found myself standing in a moment I'd experienced before—not quite a sense of *déjà vu* but of returning to something I'd known from childhood. That old sense that there is a *this,* a reality that is normal and right but is not of this world. When life departs from this reality, it is because life itself, not this reality, is somehow incomplete, imperfect—and that the *this* lies in another country than this life does. We only taste it here, but the taste is what makes survival possible.

I think we sometimes get in this life a taste of what lies in that other country. It comes back unexpected, and then for a moment we are transported—always into the same moment, a moment when we sense, however briefly and incompletely, a little of what lies on the other side of the mirror.

I'd been standing staring at the clouds longer than I thought. I can't say anything changed, either the difficulty I faced or myself, but when I walked on, my burden seemed strangely lightened and my heart was comforted.

Heavy Weather

Last evening, running an errand to a village some miles away, I drove through a drowned landscape on the turn of the season, as summer slips slowly out like the tide. The leaves are still green, but they've taken on that dusty darkness they get when their chloroplasts begin to die away. It's cooling down and the light is changing; afternoons are warm but mornings and evenings are chilly.

As I drove eastward through heavy mizzle and gusts of winds, I saw that the fields had taken on that blankly empty look they get as they settle into their winter fallow. Pooled water lay dull among the furrows and in the ditches. The sky lowered heavy, without a trace of color even though it was sunset.

To the south and east, great swirling storms are dancing their way up the seaboard in this season of hurricanes, and this heavy weather is probably the outer edge of the latest swirl of violence. We are, in this way, a little connected to the devastation elsewhere, and that's as it should be; your hurricane is my wet and windy weather.

Up here we spend much of the year ducking the climate, which can be downright ungodly. Instead of driving along a ridge road past a gravel quarry and abandoned farms as the light slipped away, I could have been in a city mall somewhere, someplace clean and brightly lit and dry, with the weather firmly excluded except when it's bright and fun and full of warmth. Could have been; was glad not to be. There was a satisfaction in the realness of this weather, in the way it connected my bit of backwoods Ontario to Florida and the Bahamas and the Carolinas and reminded me to pray for them. There is distance between this country and those, and there may be physical barriers like the sea, but the boundaries are purely artificial. Weather connects us.

One thing I like about living in a tiny, undistinguished town is the constant unstated connectedness of life, its concreteness, its realness. Welfare mothers aren't abstractions; they are friends, normal women with normal worries and very little money, and you see how their children are denied what your own children have, unthinkingly and without any real justice. If you're tempted to generalize about the poor, some known face—adult or child, woman or man—gets in the way of your abstract indignation or your well-intentioned condescension. Even the layabouts, the shiftless, the losers are *known* layabouts and shiftless and losers, and it becomes possible to understand what might have sent them spinning in that direction. It's a little harder to be thoughtlessly self-righteous when you continually trip over real, warm, living bodies.

When you see the same faces day by day, they stubbornly insist on turning human, especially when the Social Conventions insist that you make eye contact and smile slightly at everyone you pass on the street—even the tough lost ones who will not or cannot smile back. See them often enough and you start wondering what lies behind their tightly closed-off faces. You start noticing the kids who have the same tough, sealed-off look—little more than babies, some of them!—and then you start seeing the child's face in the lost adult. If you're willing to look with love and without judgment, even the faces of real losers become human, recognizable, and even oddly beautiful. You can see the faintest trace of what God sees in them. And you can see that what's in their faces hurts God's very heart for what has conspired to drive that beauty inward and underground.

Easier to keep life neat and tidily controlled; easier to stay detached and self-contained; easier not to risk rain and wind and to stay indoors with the TV on and the curtains closed. Easier to step over the drunk sleeping on the sidewalk without a second thought. Easier not to see the needs or the helplessness or the real humanity of others. Easier to focus on your particular patch of reality, with its personal comforts and discomforts, and forget about the rest.

Easier neither to give love nor to ask for it, because giving means real work and asking means taking real risks. Easier not to desire, because you may not get what you want—or worse still, you may get it and have to live up to it. Easier to ask for nothing, because if you take, you will also have to give. Easiest of all not to feel, because feeling inevitably brings pain as well as pleasure. Numbness is the easiest choice of all.

In the mall there is no rain, no wind, no lowering sky, no bitter cold or strangling heat, no thunder or freezing rain. In the mall the colors are correct and agreeable, skillfully arranged with just the right touch of glitter, and the stores are full of attractive objects that promise contentment, the good life that someone else possesses and somehow is never ours. Temperature and humidity are kept carefully in the Comfort Zone, and the lighting is steady and not too direct. Of course, there are no sunsets either, no Milky Way, nor the sort of moonlight you could almost read by, nor snowscapes strangely blue, nor fireflies and frogs and Michaelmas daisies. But we can always go outside for those when we want to, when we feel like it, if the weather's not too inconvenient, if we remember. Can't we?

Can we?

The rain thickened and the wind picked up, making my little car shudder and skip as I came back into town, running for home as the darkness rolled in. And there, blessedly familiar, were the windows of my house, all lit up and glowing warm. When you're coming from the east at evening and the lights are on, this old house always looks a little magical. Weather like this intensifies the magic, makes the light in the windows deeper and stronger, more welcoming, warmer, more richly gold.

No rain, no rainbow. No sorrow, no joy.

Non-Fiction

Hanging out laundry in a backyard full of self-seeded holly-hocks and wild grapes and milkweed plants and dragonflies. The sun is stunning, and I can hear the neighbor children playing. Next door, Sadie barks at nothing in particular. If I listen hard, I can hear a baseball game at the playing field across the creek. My hair tickles the back of my neck; sweat rolls down between my shoulder blades, and I stop to slap a mosquito.

I read an in-depth book review yesterday, of a postmodern novel, full of clever dysfunctional rich people with jobs I never heard of, behaving in self-destructive ways, facing death with a snarling stoicism that passes for courage. The reviewer praised the novel's clarity of insight and honesty about the Human Condition. It was as though, somehow, the world in the novel was the really-real world, whereas this world, the world in which I am pinning out laundry as two squirrels play-fight through the spruce tree, is somehow inadequately existent.

I am thinking, as I toss sheets on the line, how baffled and sus-picious, even contemptuous, these characters and the author and reviewer might feel about this world, this modest place of scruffy yards and apparent failure, of small sounds and quiet scents, of the constant, gentle work of living and tending and getting by, learning to be, learning to trust, learning to give and take love. What fools (they'd say) we are, to be taken in by the illusion of hope! What idiots to allow ourselves to feel and be vulnerable! What crazies to hope for love, real love, and for a life beyond the River! Obvious self-delusion; refusal to Face Facts.

But Christ faced life squarely, not stupidly—oh, not stupidly! He knew about people. Nothing and no one took him in. He had the clear, devastating sight of an illusionless child. And still illu-sionless, trusting, smart as a snake and gentle as a dove, he con-fronted the pain and walked straight at it, right through it, and out the other side.

And those who have followed him on this Way, however fool-ish they may have seemed at the time, seem to have come away with something. They have given up much that the world values; they have done the long, hard, grinding work of becoming disciplined and loving and faithful and giving people. They have chosen to live fully into each moment, *this* moment, *this* small shard of time, and have chosen God in this moment, over and over and over again. They have looked at pain and failure and deep loss and walked straight into and through them, refusing to be embittered or to return ill for ill. They have chosen to be strong in themselves but also gentle with others.

They have chosen loss and healing. We all clutch our doll-Gods, even the best of us: power or status or money, a loved place or person, our own feelings of hurt and rage, a hobby, a calling, a theory, a church, a child, a set of beliefs. And God takes these dolls away from us, gently if we'll permit, not so gently if we clutch hard. Those who follow the Way have accepted these losses, not pretending they don't hurt, but in the knowledge that there can be only one god, and that had better be God.

But at the same time, even in pain, they have chosen to move toward the Light. They have chosen to be wounded and whole, healers and healed. They have chosen to become all that God has given them to be, to move toward fullness and maturity, toward a perfection that has little to do with being "perfect" and a whole lot to do with being wholly, fully, completely human—to become as much as they can possibly be. Miraculously so.

So if they're such self-deluding dolts, these Christ-followers, why, then, can their lives flood so inexplicably, at the hardest and most painful moments, with this strange sense of peace and happiness? In what should be times of fear and anxiety, why do they feel as though they're being held so securely, so strongly, cradled in love as a child in its mother's arms? Why, when they should be mourning, do they seem suffused by a deep and trustful joy?

Why *this* Way? Because, hard as it sometimes is, it brings us to a place of light and wholeness and joy and true fulfillment. I don't think the other way has quite the same conclusion.

> But the souls of the righteous are in the hand of God.
>   and no torment will ever touch them.
> In the eyes of the foolish they seemed to have died,
>   and their departure was thought to be a disaster,

and their going forth from us to be their destruction;
　　but they are at peace.
For though in the sight of others they were punished,
　　their hope is full of immortality.
Having been disciplined a little, they will receive a great good,
　　because God tested them and found them worthy of himself;
like gold in the furnace he tried them,
　　and like a sacrificial burnt offering he accepted them.
In the time of their visitation they will shine forth,
　　and will run like sparks through the stubble.
They will govern nations and rule over peoples,
　　and the Lord will reign over them forever.
Those who trust in him will understand truth,
　　and the faithful will abide with him in love,
because grace and mercy are upon his holy ones,
　　and he watches over his elect.

(Wisdom 3:1-9, RSV)

-6-

Portraits, Chiefly Fictional

Two Geeks in Glory

[Note: Before anyone takes offense at the word "geek," it's what they call themselves with considerable pride.]

As I did the dishes, I could hear them talking: one of my dinner guests, a bright, young-adult friend whose software development company is just taking off and my older kid, Ross. My friend—call him Mike—was showing Ross the first steps in programming in Q-BASIC. Ross was responding rapidly and readily to what I knew was expert mentoring and was being a model kid to boot. The two of them were going at extremely high speed. Two geeks in glory.

It was a revelation to me. Ross and I go back a ways—thirteen years and a bit—and I thought I knew him reasonably well. I knew that the kid is a bright bulb, but now, overhearing these two, I saw the bulb with the lampshade off. I'd never really seen this aspect of his intelligence before—the way he knew intuitively how the computer's "mind" would work, predicting its logic; the way he could leap happily to the design of an algorithm like a trout leaping in midwater. There is a gift there, and it may be formidable. And more, there was a swift and happy purposefulness, a sort of rightness: a bird in the air, a horse and its rider, Ross and the computer. Ross's exchanges with the world are often tense and wary because he is not a standard-issue thirteen-year-old kid; but this may be a world where he will belong exactly as he is.

We talk about orthodox and revisionist, about stability and change, and we fail to recognize (because we aren't looking) that the world around us is not standing still. Listening to these two, who are so very much younger than I am, I realized that St. Paul could never have put "can out-intuit a CPU in Q-BASIC" into his list of gifts differing, but it *is* a gift, and one that not many have. It wouldn't have occurred to the Early Fathers that the Church could move into cyberspace. I'm trying, and failing, to imagine how St. Thomas Aquinas might react to Windows 95.

The world that Mike and Ross inhabited in such happy absorption is real, and it is only going to leap forward still further. We will be able to bring many of our inherited principles to bear in this new world; we can, and should, behave like Christians in cyberspace. Mike, most impressively, is bringing these principles to bear in managing his work force, which is stretching him considerably.

But some areas of this world simply have no counterpart in Scripture. Do we, then, put them outside the canon of our belief? Do we force them into old models, warping them badly in the process (and looking idiotic as we do so)? Or do we broaden the canon to include the new reality?

Going by the rules will only get us in trouble in this brave new world, because the rules were designed for a different world than this. Making new sets of rules isn't going to help, because the reality will change so rapidly that the new sets will be outdated as soon as we invent them. We can, of course, refuse to live with the new reality: "It worked for my grandmother, it's good enough for me." And the world will whiz past us without a second thought.

There is an alternative: we step out into cyberspace with a sense of freedom and trustfulness and even joy, and we can invite the Spirit to come along for the ride. I had the sense almost from my first baby step on the 'Net that there is serendipity out here, luck-fulness, accident, randomness, chaos, because this is a medium that none can really control. It's also a medium for playfulness. Wherever that freedom, that playfulness, is possible, and we stop trying to own and manage the whole shop, there is the opportunity for grace.

There was grace in Mike's and Ross's exchange: grace in the boy's mind leaping, grace in the young man's mentoring, grace in the ease and smoothness of their dealing, in their mutual valuing. There is grace in this strange new world if we're willing to bring the Spirit with us. There is love—very real love—among people who have never set eyes on each other in the flesh. There is care and the sense of community. And this is as real as the "real" world, and somehow we will have to stretch the fabric of our Christian tradition to enfold it. Wouldn't be the first time either. I seem to remember something about St. Paul and the Gentiles.

Of course, we'll need our continuities, too, and our ceremonies of grace. I may be sending this piece off from an IBM clone into cyberspace, but I send it from an old house full of the scent of peonies. Mike may be managing a leading-edge computer firm, but he's doing so with a set of very old-fashioned principles rooted firmly in the Gospel. Ross may eventually leap into serious programming, but he will, I hope, take his traditions with him.

But leap these young ones will. And who will leap with them?

Two Women—Part 1

She (who is a composite of several women I have known) never, never gets angry. She accepts that life has its angles and edges, that sometimes it bruises her and hers, but when this happens, she takes an attitude ranging from resigned humor to mild exasperation at worst. And then she marches on regardless, always cheerful, always forgiving.

She says herself that she knows she's too sensitive; cruel comments hurt her deeply, and she hates fights. She herself is not a critical person, and she finds it necessary to avoid critical people, because she has such trouble with their unkindness. Love is all that matters, and love is unconditional, positive regard. It has been said of her that trying to fight with her is like trying to fight with a feather pillow, except feather pillows don't dissolve into floods of tears.

To her, it is important to be kind, to be nurturing, to be supportive, to be accepting. This is how she sees herself, and the more she follows this pattern, the happier she is with herself, the more content she is in her own skin.

Such a good woman, and so nice—until the pressure builds too far or something hurts her where she really lives; then she has literally no way of releasing her anger properly. And so it leaks out around the edges in rather frightening ways. Because she's good at getting people to confide in her, she knows where the vulnerable spots are, and under the right circumstances she will go for them. Moreover, because she has never learned to be properly angry, she uses passive aggression, which is deadly dangerous—far worse than real anger because it saws its opponent off at the ankles. Passive aggression can't be fended off, because it's so confusing and doesn't look like anger at all; it's poison, sugar-coated. And finally, because she is so invested in being a good, nice, kind woman, her anger, when it comes, will be wrapped in impenetrable self-righteousness. It will be unanswerable, it will be expressed in sweetly loving terms, and it will go right to the bone and hurt like the very devil. But she will be utterly unaware of what she has done, because she never, ever feels anger.

Anger is a normal part of human nature, and we'd better learn to live with it. If we're very, very lucky, life will give us few occasions for real anger, and it helps enormously if we learn not to take offense easily—a matter of growing a good tough hide, exercising common sense, and not ascribing the worst to other people. But I doubt if one person gets through life without having something to get really, truly mad about. And that's the rub.

The way to deal with anger is to express it honestly, confront whatever the angry-making thing is (ideally, within ourselves), and then let go of the angry-making thing and get on with life instead of obsessing about it. Usually we don't do this because we're afraid of the confrontation part—afraid of standing up, when that's necessary, afraid of confronting whatever-it-is inside that's been so badly jangled, afraid we'll just get mashed flat if we say anything, afraid that God will not forgive us for being less than perfect and getting mad in the first place.

If we don't know how to handle anger, we're apt to err in one of two ways: to become too aggressive or to become too passive. Too aggressive flies off the handle easily, takes snits, flies into unwarrantable rage, does preemptive attacks, goes ballistic, turns abusive. Too passive takes revenge in much sneakier and quite unpleasant ways by ever-so-gently going for the other party's ego, doing a great deal of subtle, almost unnoticeable, but very deep damage.

This failure comes from our inability to embrace the central paradox of Christianity: that God is indeed both loving and judging—loving us and judging others, judging us and loving others. We want the first of those two, but not the second. We want Jesus to be the tender shepherd to us, not the strong-minded prophet being rude to Pharisees and heaving around tables in the Temple in very real anger. Or we want Jesus to be the stern authority confronting sin, but not the man who looks at the miserable schlemiel next to us with such understanding and compassion and delight, holding his arms out to the prodigal. We want to be seen as loving and accepting or as tough and realistic, and we reject the other half of the equation as spiritually inadequate. But that's our failure, not God's.

The great virtue of Christianity is that it allows us to be sinners. It sets a tough standard coupling honesty and love, love and honesty. We invariably wobble badly at toeing this line, simply because we are human. If we don't accept that failure, that humanity, in ourselves, it's because we're not looking too closely at our own behavior—usually because we're having much too much fun jumping on someone else's. It says something that this nice woman almost always speaks of others with condescension.

Life hurts; life is difficult; life is not always fair; life has the capacity to make us angry, and anger can become a sin—something parting us and those around us from God's love. It can do so as the Sin of Anger, festering resentment like a boil; or it can do so as the Inverse Sin of Anger, passive aggression masking really deep anger by niceness.

We're meant to see ourselves as Miserable Offenders, not because God insists that we're nogoodniks, but because it's always much better to have one's sins up front, where one can keep an eye on them, than to stow them out of sight, where they can get away with murder. This nice woman—and she really is a nice woman, by the way, genuinely kind and loving—has set her quite real aggressive streak off to one side, where she doesn't have to look at it honestly and be responsible for it, and it bites people while she keeps her back carefully turned on it. But we don't tame our dragons by turning our backs on them. We tame them by facing them squarely, naming their names, calling them our own.

Much better, I think, to lay her need for niceness and sweetness-and-light on the altar as a sacrifice and honestly to accept her own real and full humanity, spots and all. That would be true self-love, the foundation of all real love for others.

Two Women—Part 2

She holds her small, neatly groomed dark head very straight on her sturdy neck, with her chin well up and her shoulders always squared. She is sensible, practical, a manager—brisk and honest, perhaps a bit too tough sometimes, but since she's genuinely kind and helpful, that's not so hard to live with. She's gutsy. She puts a whole lot of value in her ability to carry the load without bending and to take on one more package for someone else, somehow getting it all done. She does a wonderful job at pastoral care for the elderly, especially those with senile dementia. They can scream at her all they please; she just shrugs and goes on "doing" for them deftly and with care. She is very good at letting things run off her back.

The only thing that's a bit odd about her is a sort of intensity, which some people have trouble dealing with—a sort of over-eagerness, as though there's a good hot fire banked down under her apparent coolness, a deep tension. She can come on awfully strong, and that gets her in trouble with gentler souls. She smokes (she's tried to give up many times) and goes through a lot of coffee (that's probably where the hand tremor comes from).

I didn't hear the stories from her, but indirectly. They're bad stories, real horrors: she was a nurse in 'Nam and saw things she cannot speak about. Her beloved brother died tragically. A bad marriage, a string of miscarriages, a bankruptcy—some have it harder than others, and she has had it very hard indeed. You'd never be able to tell from her bearing and briskly cheerful manner.

She has borne a great deal, far too much, and she has borne it proudly, in a disciplined way, looking after others and keeping her own needs to herself. She's tough, and she takes pride in that. She knows that she can walk through the Valley of the Shadow of Death, leading a whole party of tenderfeet, and find fruit in the desert to sustain them all.

After I'd heard the stories, I could look at her a little differently. I could begin to feel the darkness in her, not of evil—not in the least!—but of a whole vat of very old pain boiled down to a thick, dark, and potent syrup. I saw her terrible perfectionist streak that will never let her off the hook, and a lurking deep anger that has nowhere to go. If she can be shrewd and incisive, that has nothing on her relentless self-criticism. She is kind and caring of others, but she will accept no care for herself. Try to touch her, and she'll flinch away and put the walls up higher.

I'd admired her coolness and self-possession. She never cries, not even when any human would; disaster just makes her calmer and more practical. Now that I know a little more, I'm not sure whether this is because she does not know how to cry or because she's so afraid that if once she started to cry, she would never be able to stop.

Her response to life has always been to set her head higher, square her shoulders more firmly, to become more capable, to feel less . . . and now she's wrapped in her rigid discipline, her over-powering strength, her deep loneliness, her stoicism, like a knight encased in armor. What lies within (I suspect, I sense) is such pain, such anger, such banked-up grief and need and longing, that I think she is terrified at what would come spilling out if anything happened to break her shell.

Once or twice she's let things drop about her faith—not often. She's old-fashioned; she was brought up to believe that faith is a private thing, something not to be spoken of. But the odd comment makes me think that hers is a stern and demanding God, with high expectations, a God who is easily ticked off. The one time I saw her really flustered was when she'd forgotten a particular prayer on her prayer list; the intention wasn't enough. Her imperfection appalled her. How *could* she have forgotten?

I wonder if she feels that if she let God at what's locked on her inside, where the pain and the pressure are, God would judge her. Or perhaps God's mercy would break her open, and the dark stuff would come spilling out, a scalding tide, hurting or appalling anyone it touched. I don't think she trusts anyone, God included, to look on that pool of darkness in her with pity and love. I think the pain of that pity and love would be more than she could bear.

Has it, I wonder, occurred to her that, in fact, God might just possibly use a person like her with enormous gentleness and tenderness and care? That seeing the darkness and where it comes from, seeing it with nothing but an ache of love, God might take it into God's own self, absorbing it for her and setting her free of it? For this was Christ's gift to us from the cross: the surety that God sees and accepts and loves us, our darkness and deep pain and all. And if God can love us, surely so can we? At least a little?

I'm not sure she could learn that lesson all at once. It's too hard for her, goes too much against her experience of life. She needs to allow the Spirit's softening touch to work on her weather-beaten soul, working in love a little at a time, whatever she could accept, like oil rubbed into cracked and calloused skin. There are layers and layers of dry toughness that need to slough off, allowing God's healing to enter, slowly, no more than she can manage at once.

All she has to do is to put aside her independence, her pride, her self-sufficiency, her strength and courage and toughness and stoicism—all the qualities she prides in herself. They were good qualities, but they stand between her and Love now. All she has to do is to hold out her deep fearfulness and anger and pain to the God who already sees and knows and loves it all. She needs to ask to be held and cherished as a child again, resting quiet and cuddling in its mother's arms. But for her, that too is so very hard. It's not something she's used to. It's even a little frightening.

God comes to us when and as he sees us ready to accept him. He does not break us when we cannot afford to be broken. Instead, if we will simply turn blindly into his arms, rooting for love like a nurseling for the breast, then he will draw us into himself, wrap us in warmth, enfolding us, softening us a little at a time, keeping it bearable, until we are ready to let go and to let his love break through in all its sharp sweetness and shining.

Speak No Evil

Let's call her Janet. See her at my kitchen table one morning, a plump, pretty woman in her thirties with soft light-brown hair, having a cup of tea and a good cry.

She had found herself caught in one of those awful situations that we all bounce into from time to time. Innocent behavior had been misinterpreted; accusations had been made, not to Janet's face but behind her back. She had been gently but quite effectively slandered. Her standing in the community had been damaged. Friends and colleagues, people she cared about, had been ready to think the worst about her without even hearing her side of the story. One or two had shunned her, and that hurt.

And there was absolutely nothing she could do. The persons responsible for misinterpreting her behavior weren't prepared to sit down and talk things out, or to give her a chance to defend herself, or to retract what they had said. The fact that no one would accuse her to her face meant that she had no official knowledge of what was going on. It was like trying to do battle with fog.

It's fine for people like me to assure Janet that this too will pass and to tell her to keep her chin up and ignore what was being said, that as long as her conscience was clean, nothing else mattered. Her conscience was clean, but she felt besmirched. Janet is a sensitive woman and a person with a formidable sense of integrity and honor. She was struggling not only with the injustice but with the huge injustice of having to swallow injustice in silence. That's a killer.

She was struggling, too, with the sense that she was making a mountain out of a molehill. As a Christian, she felt that she should be tougher-skinned and quick to forgive. Our Lord, after all, had faced huge injustice in silence and had gone to a totally undeserved death without saying a word. Her reaction seemed invalid to her; she could not forgive herself for caring so much about something that should matter so little.

She was hurt, but she was also angry. She needed to hear that her hurt and anger were legitimate, that our feelings do matter and have to be dealt with, although we must always try to be careful about how we act and what we say. She needed to realize that just because we're Christians, we can't always be saints. She needed, too, to talk out possible courses of action and decide what to do.

I let her talk things out. Sometimes there's nothing else to do. We can't always wrestle Wrong to the mat and make it cry "Uncle!" Sometimes we just have to live with it, talk it out over and over, learn what we can from it, and then shrug and walk away. And sometimes this will mean that we have to shrug and walk away from people when they're too much in love with their own opinions to listen to us. That, too, is a difficult decision if we take our faith seriously, because it goes against the grain.

Evil exists. We tend to see it in large, horrible, blatant situations, like Bosnia and Rwanda; or we watch *Schindler's List* and confront the horrors of the Holocaust. But evil also has a tendency to thread its way into our lives in small, terribly damaging ways. Those who had slandered Janet were merely succumbing to ordinary human nature. It almost certainly didn't occur to them that their behavior had hurt her terribly; and quite possibly, they would have shrugged and accused her of "overreacting" for being so hurt. (That, too, was something she realized and that hobbled her. "Sensitive" is a dirty word in our culture, and a sense of honor is positively Victorian.)

And evil, sadly, is terribly contagious. Most likely the people responsible for slandering Janet were operating out of the evil done to them by other people, because that's usually the pattern. The abused become abusers, the hurt inflict hurt, gossip begets gossip. In small and insignificant ways, as well as in large ones, we are the products of our own history.

Janet will be fine, because she's a figment of my imagination, a composite of a number of individuals, male and female, past and present. But pray for the real Janets, because they do exist. Pray also for those responsible for the wrong inflicted on the Janets. And speak no evil, for when you do, you grieve our God.

Dolores

Annie had been away from the Stitch and Bitch Club (that's what they call their weekly handicraft group) for more than a month before the newest member, Dolores, asked why she'd dropped out. The other women looked at each other. "Personal reasons," Carol said.

"Oh, you mean the miscarriage."

"Well, that . . . But also they're on a tight budget and you know what materials cost."

"Oh, I'm sure she could find the money if she really wanted to. Look at us—we thought we'd have to cancel the trip to Bermuda because of Alison's braces, but I just jiggled the budget."

"I don't think there's much budget to jiggle any more," Karen said, with an edge in her voice. "Bill's been laid off for months."

"Is that why they put their house on the market? It's such a silly time to try to sell the place; they should wait until spring, when the market's better." Dolores was off and running. "It's just as well then, isn't it, that she lost the baby? I mean, three kids already and one more mouth to feed, and now maybe she can go out and look for a job. There must be something she can do— babysitting or waiting tables or something—and Bill could look after the kids. Look at all the ads in the paper. All these unemployed people—I think they just don't have the gumption to go out and find work. When my oldest boy—he's a software engineer—lost his job, he found another one within a week. And Bill's a trucker, there should be lots of things he can do. Though didn't I see something in the paper about the trucking industry? Anyway, people just have to have enough determination. And they've got to manage their money sensibly. I mean, you *can* eat hamburger, can't you? You don't have to have steak. I'm very careful; I always watch prices and sales, and I always buy in bulk when the prices are good. Which reminds me, there's a sale on at the Bay. They've got those beautiful fine percale sheets for half-price, only fifty dollars a set or something. You girls might want to take a look. I've found you can pick up some real bargains at places like the Sally Ann if you get there before the welfare mums. I got Alison a lovely Harris tweed coat there, just as good as new, and it was only thirty-five dollars. Which reminds me, she doesn't like the color so I suppose I should take it back. And I keep an eye on auctions and garage sales and things. I found the loveliest old pine table at an auction for only a hundred fifty dollars. You wouldn't believe what it looks like now that I've had it refinished. Anyway, I'm sure they'll get by nicely if they're sensible. People do, don't they?"

The others kept their eyes on their work and their thoughts to themselves. Dolores gathered up her macrame. "Well, girls, I suppose I'd better get going; I've got a lot of shopping to do. Does anyone have a really good recipe for lemon shrimp? No? Well, I'll think of something. Bye-bye. See you next Wednesday."

When she was gone, they looked at each other. Carol said, "Why don't we meet at my place next week, just for a change? After all, poor Joan's been hosting the group for months. And maybe we could meet at Karen's the week after that."

"We must remember to tell Dolores."

"Yes, we must, mustn't we?"

Part 3

"sleep jesus on the stones"

holy saturday

sleep Jesus on the stones beneath your skin
the winding sheet not warm enough to warm your bones

rest Jesus while the blood that oozed from those unholy holy wounds
turns black and crumbles like the clods of earth on which it fell

stay Jesus hold us numb in the embrace of your unlovely lovely dying
while we who shiver here in hell
wait for your rising for your leaving
for our waiting
for the filling of the hollow space with hope

—Allen Stairs

-7-

Living in Sin

Mr. Rabin

(written after the Quebec referendum and the assassination of Israel's prime minister)

Mr. Rabin is dead tonight, and the reason is fear and hatred.

It is terribly easy (as my own country has discovered yet again in the last week) to define US in terms of THEM. WE are special, set apart, holy, right, ordained of God; THEY are trying to undermine us, undercut us, give away our rights, take over our culture. WE are Good; THEY are Bad. WE are saints; THEY are sinners.

It almost doesn't matter who THEY are. Maudits anglophones, if you're in Trois-Rivières; Quebec frogs if you're from Brockville, Ontario. The PLO if you're a right-wing Israeli; the Jewish oppressors if you're a Palestinian. Bosnians if you're a Serb, Serbs if you're a Bosnian. Hutus and Tutsis, Commie pinkos, bleeding hearts, right-wing bigots, homophobes, fruits, feminist bitches, male-chauvinist-sexist-oinkers . . . name your poison.

The fact is that each and every one of us is beloved by God, known, seen, treasured, hoped for, by God. Therefore, when I judge and reject you or you judge and reject me, for whatever reason, we are doing violence to God's love for each other as individuals, and we are grieving God terribly.

The person who shot and killed Rabin was "hating the sin" of Rabin's "betrayal" of Israel's interests by negotiating with the PLO.

His motive was utterly pure, in that sense. It seems to me that hatred is often far more pure than love. Hatred is clean and simple, while love is muddled and messy. Hatred sees clear and simple black-and-white; love sees a hopeless confusion of greys. Hatred goes for simple causes and answers and solutions; love wrings its hands trying to figure out what's best for the other. Hatred is easy. Love is the hardest work in the world.

The hard thing now is to see that young man, the one who killed Rabin, and to understand that he, too, is God's beloved child and to try to understand why he acted as he did. Which doesn't mean letting him off the hook. Forgiveness does not mean "no consequences." But it does mean grappling with the underlying causes of his act, just as we in Canada must now truly grapple with the problems we face, instead of trying to dodge them.

The older I get, the more complex and difficult life becomes. But I would not have it otherwise.

Hell's Bells

According to my Saturday paper, the Church of England has just issued a report saying that "although traditional images of hell as an eternal torment are wrong, everyone will still face a Day of Judgement." No problems there.

I guess the question is: How many chances does God give us? Is there some point at which we're faced for the umpteenth time with the choice of accepting God's true insight and intensity of love, but we turn away for the umpteenth-and-one time (because genuine love is scary stuff), and God says, "Right, go be like that" and gives up on us? That just doesn't feel intuitively right to me. God is love.

On the other hand, personal experience says that while love doesn't give up on the other person, sometimes the other person gives up on accepting love. To accept that we're loved, truly loved just as we are, we have to accept that the other person really *sees* us, and that can take more self-confidence than we have. Accepting love means accepting our own imperfections and failings; and the more love we accept, the more strength and courage we have to do that.

But some folks seem not to be able to do this; they put their own need to feel good about themselves first. Sit down with such a person and you'd find that she sees nothing wrong with herself at all. He can't understand why he runs into such problems, when he is really such a good and likeable person. She wallows in self-pity a fair bit. He is intensely sensitive to criticism, while being exceptionally hardhearted about others. She shies away from the tough, hard work of growth and relatedness because that hurts. He is deeply, deeply hurt when his wife lays charges of assault: "How could you be so disloyal?" At the end Hitler was profoundly sorry for himself and saw only what he had done for Germany and how Germany had betrayed him.

To these people, facing God's real love is absolutely terrifying, because it strips away their illusions about themselves and leaves them unbeautifully naked and exposed, looking Love in the face and knowing exactly how badly they've blown it. Maybe even then they can be healed and turned to God. But maybe they turn away and flee into chaos and nothingness. Maybe the Church of England is right. Wouldn't be the first time. But if that's what happens, I'm willing to bet that it's *their* choice, that annihilation, not God's.

We cannot know what's going to lie on the other side of the River or what awaits us at the Day of Judgment. The one thing I am sure of, however, is that God's eye, when it regards us, is full of deep love—and of even deeper pain when we turn our backs on love.

Hot Potato

This is how it happens.

"If I have to face what I did, which I know is wrong, it will shame me, and that shame will be painful, and I fear that pain. So I'll deny that I did anything wrong and play hot potato with guilt. The snake made me do it!"

"If I have to face change, I know I will have to change myself, and changing myself will be painful, and I fear that pain. So I will refuse to change, and I will say that I am being firm in my principles."

"If I have to face uncertainty, it will mean puzzling and agonizing over my decisions instead of simply following The Rules. And that's a whole lot of work and worry and trouble. I'm afraid of that. I might make mistakes. So I'll put everything in black and white and say that the alternative is chaos and relativism."

"If I have to face the homeless person or the poor or the deprived child, I will have to give up some of the good things I enjoy, and giving up will be painful, and I fear that pain. So I will be an individualist and fight for my right to keep every penny of what I earn."

"If I must listen to and try to comfort another person in pain, I won't know what to do or say, and I'm afraid I'll feel inadequate. So I'll cross the street or change the subject or block the flow with a plug of Good Advice or small talk, or do anything so that I do not have to take some of that pain into myself. And I will call that protecting my privacy."

"If I have to face what was done to me, the abuse I suffered, then I will have to experience real agony, and I fear that pain. So I will pass on to others what was done to me; I will treat the other person as a thing, not a person. And I will call this being tough."

"If I have to face the fact that I have wounded another person and accept the pain of that knowledge, it will hurt. I'm afraid of how I would feel about myself. So I will hate and blame my victim and justify my own behavior. I will call this exposing evil and facing the facts."

"If I have to live in real connectedness with another person, to learn real love, I will have to face the fact that I can be vulnerable and needy and dependent and weak and in desperate need of tenderness, and I'm afraid of being like that, because that just gets you hurt. So I will run away from love and hide, although I know that hurts the other. And I will call this being strong and independent."

"If I have to face what I have done to others, I will have to accept my own wrongness and hurtfulness, and that will hurt terribly. That's terrifying. So I will put on blinkers and not look at what I do. After all, good self-esteem is very important."

"If I accept that I am loved and lovable, that I am God's precious child, I will have to learn to stand up to injustice, and that means I may get hurt. There will be conflict, and I hate conflict. I'm afraid of fighting. Sometimes it's easier to be a doormat. I will call this being gentle and looking after others."

"If I am to let go of what I passionately desire, it's going to hurt. I fear that loss. Easier to plunge on pursuing what I want, whatever it costs, and to call that firmness of purpose."

"If I am to trust in God, I will have to step out into what feels like emptiness, and that is frightening. So I will try to manage and control everything myself, and I will call that being responsible."

"If I am to ask for healing, I have to admit that I need it, and that means looking honestly at the past and revisiting real pain, and that scares me. So I will insist that I don't have any problems and can take my licks, and I will call that being strong and stoical."

"If I am to accept God's love, I am going to have to accept God's very clear vision of just who I am, and that is truly terrifying, because God is so good and I am so not-very-good. Easier to accept God as judgmental and rule-bound, or to turn my back on God completely. A truly loving God is the most terrifying thing of all."

No wonder God weeps . . .

Christ managed somehow to stare down his very human fear and to walk straight through it on the way to the Cross, to show us once and for all that there is nothing, nothing at all, to fear from the fullness of love. We too will find the courage, if we're willing to believe and to trust in love when we're faced with fear and pain. God cups us so tenderly in the palm of his hand, seeing us with such perfect clearness, and loving us so dearly; all he wants is for us to accept that love—to allow ourselves to be loved and to love in return.

Bread and Stones

I don't have my Dorothy Parker omnibus anymore, but I remember a sweet, quiet, truly vicious four-line epitaph she wrote for a woman who had insisted on "giving bread / When all they asked was stones." In dear Mrs. Parker's eyes, this woman clearly was a fool for loving people who didn't want to be loved.

On a less nasty level, Miss Manners would characterize the woman's behavior as . . . unfortunate, perhaps a little self-indulgent, and inconsiderate of the feelings of the recipient. We should give others what they want, not what we want to give them, Miss Manners would murmur gently. Insisting on handing someone a good loaf of French bread when all that person wants is a rock is a little presumptuous on our part. It has been recorded, she would note, that a person who is the object of unrequited love is almost as uncomfortable as the person doing the unrequited loving.

But against this, we're given the New Testament directions. Love, and keep on loving. Give, and keep on giving. Don't ever give up. We have the Beatitudes (Matthew 5:3-12), and as one Anglican commentator observed, the Beatitudes are God's instructions to us to behave in ways that the world finds distinctly loopy. Blessed are the meek? Are you kidding? Do you want to get pounded into applesauce on life's playground?

And the fact is that we do have to live in this world, we do have to survive, and for that reason we sometimes have to compromise. It's in the Next World, not in this one, that God's Word is to be lived out perfectly. God made us to be his children, not doormats; and Miss Manners' position on the bread/rock business does have some validity. Nonetheless, the basic instructions seem to be clear. Whatever Mrs. Parker and Miss Manners think, we are supposed to keep trying to hand out bread, not rocks. Even if sometimes we feel like complete fools for being like this.

For the fact is that we all need love, even if we'd prefer not to admit that to ourselves or others. We all need to be fed, even if our pride would have us deny that we're hungry. We need interconnection with others, even if we fear and dislike it. We are pulled toward God because we need love and nourishment, and we are pulled away from God because we fear being dependent and needy and facing others' dependency and neediness.

Feeding each other the bread of love and accepting this food from others' hands is what God wants to see happening, although we find it surprisingly tough going a lot of the time. It takes courage to accept that we aren't perfect; it takes radical courage to accept that we are loved.

Blessed are those who have chosen the other path, the one that involves admitting that we don't have it together, that we are vulnerable. It's the harder path, this one—the Journey in Faith—but it has the greater rewards in the end. It is those who are hurting, uncertain, questioning, exploring, those who have learned how to be compassionate, who are most apt to know that they need feeding with the bread of God's love and who pass on that bread to others.

Strong-Minded (January 6)

It is a grand and terrible thing to have a very strong will.

I speak as one who has a will about the size of a Percheron. I don't want much, but when I really want something, I REALLY want it with every fiber of myself. I may pretend to be patient and forbearing, but underneath the patience my will is straining at the leash—and this comes out in ways that don't make me happy with myself. Over-intensity, snapping at my children, compulsive behavior. I end up upsetting myself and everyone else within earshot. And when I get like this, whatever-it-is I'm after is invariably not in the cards for me. The more I want something, the less apt I am to receive it, which makes for a whole lot of pain and frustration in my life. Because, for a smart person, I can be awful dumb sometimes, it wasn't until the last time this happened that I finally twigged to the underlying message.

God does not want me to worship anything or anybody but God.

Worship comes from "worth-ship," giving worth to something. If I put something (or somebody) in the center of my universe, focus on wanting and needing it, turn all that Percheron of a will in that direction, then I am displacing God, who *should* be at the center of my universe. This is a very human tendency on my part, and because I am a strong-willed person, God has to get exceedingly tough with me about it. Sort of like the prospector's mule: I sometimes need a whack upside the head with a two-by-four just to get my attention.

Well, I just got another whack, and this time, Sir or Madam, I'm inclined to feel that You were in the right, and I'm sorry, and in the future I shall try to remember Who should come first with me, and I hope You will forgive me and allow me to undo the damage I did.

The light dawns. Oh—right. Epiphany!

The Three-Toed One

This has been a great week for Sloth.

Started Monday afternoon with a painful parent-teacher-child meeting concerning younger son's (non)work habits. Serial work emergencies throughout the week caused by dilatory clients. Penitential meeting with bank person on Wednesday about my bad habit of putting off dealing with bank-type stuff. On Friday the daughter of a workaholic friend (Inverse Sloth, there) finally *really* went off the rails, largely because daddy has been ducking dealing with her for years.

Most of us can see that there really is something Wrong with self-centered Pride, and pervasive, corrosive Anger (usually self-righteous) is also pretty unappealing. We don't mind jumping on Lust, Covetousness, and Envy. Gluttony looks appealing when it involves chocolate truffles, but mostly we know that it is the one of the Seven Daddies most likely to kill us, as well as being bad for the figure. So why do we think Sloth is cute?

But we do. And it isn't. My younger kid has been sliding through school, quietly circling Saturn instead of doing his work, and he's probably going to repeat Grade 4. Our clients shrug and smile and pass on their mismanagement of their time to us, charmingly asking us to meet unbeatable deadlines just for them, and our families pay as our stress level rises and we work through weekends. I'm adorably "awful with money," and I'm not in real trouble with the bank yet, this being a small town and forgiving, but I could easily be in deep if I don't pull up my socks. And a certain young lady will pay dearly for her father's ostrich-like approach to parenting.

Sloth isn't cute. Scott Peck identifies inertia as the root of all evil, which is probably a bit of an exaggeration, but not much.

I do see the need for tradition, conservatism, caution; it does not behoove us, individually or corporately, to hop on our hobbyhorses and ride wildly off in all directions. But neither are we to rest on our keisters on the Journey in Faith. If we are spiritually living, stasis is out of the question; it's not okay to stay where we are. It's either onward or downward, increased life or death. Because living things must grow or die. Souls included.

I had reason to look up one of the parables in Matthew, the rather harsh and puzzling one about the master and the three servants (Matthew 25:14-30). Two servants doubled the money their master had left them to manage. The third buried his thousand gold coins (thereby, under Jewish law, offloading any responsibility for what happened to the money). When the boss got back, the risk-taking two were praised and rewarded; the cautious sloth got a tongue-lashing and the bum's rush. The parable ends with the apparently harsh comment that those who already have something will get more, while those who have little will lose even that.

Which seems very uncharitable, until you think of it in terms of spiritual growth. I could take my soul and bury it, refusing to grow and change, refusing to become a mature and loving person. In effect, I would be refusing to take the responsibility for making the most of my me-ness, whatever is at the center of Molly. Then my soul would do no growing, and in the end, what I would get to present to God when I meet him is a shriveled little pickle of a soul instead of the fine, full-grown fruit that he expects. I've seen the results of spiritual Sloth up close, and they are not pretty.

Or we can take the harder, riskier path toward growth and change, increasing responsibility, increasing maturity, doubling our capacity for love (which is, I admit, a very painful process!) but growing, learning, increasing in strength and capacity and endurance. It's an energetically expensive process, given our natural tendency to want to stay in one spot (or possibly even slide backward).

But ultimately this soul-growing is very satisfying, with the possibility of true joy, real love, if we're willing to stretch for it, do the work—above all, if we're willing to take the risk of moving on, stepping out into thin air, trusting that either the ground will be there under our feet or that we will be taught how to fly.

A Mouse Up My Nose
(a Lenten meditation on sin and forgiveness)

This all came up a few years ago, when I was trying to figure out how to deal with Rhoda. Rhoda (not her real name) was a fellow parishioner with a serious obsession about the rector, who, Rhoda felt, could do no right. It got bad enough that most of us would duck down the next aisle in the supermarket or nip down side streets or dive into wholly inappropriate stores whenever we saw Rhoda coming. Talk about mosquitos! I had picked up the clue that Rhoda's relationship with her own father had been the Pits, and it takes very little cleverness to think "Aha! psychological transference!" which made Rhoda's behavior more understandable but certainly not bearable.

She had trapped me in the frozen food aisle one day, metaphorically pinning me up against the french fries and railing on about poor old Father X, when suddenly an image popped fullblown into my head. Not, perhaps, a pleasant or savory image, but one that at least made me giggle internally.

Dealing with Rhoda's obsession was like having a dead mouse shoved up my nose.

We all get faced with intolerable behavior sometimes, just as we all commit intolerable behavior sometimes. Dealing with the latter is at least straightforward if you're a grown-up and a Christian. You apologize, you take your Consequences like a good soldier, you try to make amends; if there are pieces to pick up, you help pick up the pieces, and you resolve to make new and fresh mistakes in the future instead of boring yourself and others by repeating the same old, tired ones. Or, if need be, you get some help because you don't seem to be able to stop repeating the same old, tired ones. Above all, however, you ask God to forgive you because you are a Miserable Offender (hereafter M.O.) (Of course, if you're not a grown-up or a Christian, your response is apt to be nowhere near this spiritually wholesome, but that's a different meditation.)

But what, as Christians, are we supposed to do when someone shoves a dead mouse up our nose? Yes, I know all this business about "forgive us our sins as we forgive others who sin against us."

I agree firmly with forgiveness, but I also believe that we do have the right, indeed the obligation, to protect our nasal passages from murine invasion. It is not good for abusive people to go on being abusive; not only is it hell for their victims, but it's bad for their own long-term psycho-spiritual well-being. I also don't hold with "forgiveness" when it's chickening out of dealing with reality.

Finally, I'm not talking about Judgment and Forgiveness and Last Things here; ultimately the only soul I can be responsible for is my own. And judgment really is God's, because God is the only person with all the evidence. With those caveats, there's still the Big Question: How am I, as someone who's practicing to be a Christian, going to get through ordinary life without making like a doormat? This is purest pragmatism: What about that mouse?

First, there's the inevitable call for prayerful discernment <sigh>—all that hard work . . . There's the difference between what people do and who they are. We can hold another person responsible for his or her actions, but not for being, say, unforgivably different from our own (of course!) naturally perfect selves. Sort that one out and get rid of it first off. That's not a dead mouse at all.

Second, a proper evaluation. There's a major difference between an isolated boo-boo and repeated offenses, between accidental and intentional, between well-meaning mistakes and serious bad behavior, and between people who say "Oops, sorry, I shouldn't have done that" and people who say "Mouse? What mouse? Do you see a mouse? I don't see a mouse."

Then there is the difficult balance between what's best for the party of the second part and what's best for me. There is the nature of the offense (the size of the mouse) and the way in which it has been pushed up one's nose. All these factors must be considered carefully and prayerfully. And then—but only after careful reflection!—comes action.

The first step, of course, is to remove the tiny corpse, holding it delicately by the tail between thumb and forefinger. The best outcome is to give it a decent burial, with a prayer, handing its mousy little soul over to God, keeping in memory the dead mice that we M.O.s have inflicted on other people's nasal passages, and accepting the human-ness of the whole process, ourselves included.

—————

This is what our Lord calls for. I think it's only reasonable to acknowledge somewhere in all this that that mouse HURT. It always does, after all, and sometimes quite badly.

There will, however, be times when we can't be perfectly forgiving, or at least not just yet, which is also part of our status as M.O.s. And there are also times when the party of the second part does need to feel a gentle Consequence or two in order not to repeat this behavior in the future.

It is acceptable, I think, under these circumstances, to hand the wee, limp corpse back to the party of the second part, saying politely, "Here, bucky, I do believe this is yours." Note that you are not supposed to throw the mouse in the offender's face or get all furiously self-righteous or get out your baseball bat and pound the offender (or the mouse) into applesauce. Just hand the danged rodent back, saying nicely but firmly: "*Your* mouse."

I finally did this to Rhoda, and now I don't dread seeing her in the supermarket anymore; we nod and smile politely as we pass. But still, some days as I pass through the frozen food aisle, I see Rhoda descend upon some other poor, unresisting soul, her eye aglitter, and a limp and skinny tail dangling from the hand clenched behind her back . . .

Lizzie Baxter

My friend Caro has just checked in to tell me how the Baxter family is doing. Their sixteen-year-old daughter Lizzie died tonight when the van she was driving hit a patch of black ice and spun out of control. Her aunt's car, which by sheer, horrible chance was oncoming in the other lane, plowed into the van. Lizzie died as her mother stood by, unable to get into the locked and shattered vehicle and reach her child.

ANY death is tragic; any death of a child is doubly tragic. There are circumstances here which I won't relate but which make my gut twist in pain for Lizzie's mother Lynn, because I too have children, and I cannot, cannot imagine anything worse than what she is going through tonight.

I can't wrestle with this as the Problem of Evil. It's not Evil; it's physics—mass times acceleration plus friction (lack of) plus . . . oh, you can see the vector arrows painting trajectories, you could measure the impact. No comfort there. No comfort in the bromides. How could I possibly offer Lizzie's mother the Standard Pieties? Not tonight. Not for a long time.

Where there is some comfort is in one piece of knowledge.

I live in a small, totally undistinguished, slightly grotty, unremarkable community, which is very, very good at grief. We've buried a number of teenagers in the last few years—several killed in road accidents and one shattering murder—and each time, what's come across is the community's utter willingness to take a piece of the pain and bear it away.

Community is the willingness to bear someone else's grief, to accept it, take it into your own bones, bear it away, feel it again. All around this town and out in the boonies around us a handful of households tonight will be trying to take some of the burden of grief off Lizzie's family's shoulders, in the (perhaps misguided) notion that sharing their load may help them.

Tomorrow, as the news spreads through the community, the grief will, I hope and pray, be shared into smaller pieces and sent from one house to the next . . . I don't know if this really works. I don't have the courage to ask. I just hope, somehow, that it helps.

"Surely he has borne our griefs and carried our sorrows." I don't know if the cry I had in the kitchen over Lizzie's death will help Lynn and David and the boys. I can only hope.

Pray for them.

Of Spiders

The big spider took up residence in my kitchen window a few days ago. It's a real beauty—almost half an inch long, with a strongly spotted abdomen and handsomely striped legs—although I must say its web is rather sloppy. Clearly it's not one of the master web-builder species. In fact, I couldn't name its genus or species to save my soul, but I do like having it around. It's a quiet companion.

This morning, as I was making coffee, I saw that it had a moth in hand, or rather in jaw, and was readying the thing for packaging, storage, and consumption. And I remembered Robert Frost's poem about the white spider on the white flower, holding a white moth, with its strong undertheme of the Problem of Evil: "What but design of darkness to appall?—If design govern in a thing so small."

Seems unfair to spiders, that poem. This animal is merely responding instinctively to the touch of dinner on its web. Spiders, like nature itself, are neither kindly nor unkindly. There is no intention in them. They merely act, quite elegantly, just as gravity acts elegantly when someone falls off a cliff, or inertia acts elegantly when two cars collide, or the cancer cell's elegant self-reproductive machinery switches into mistaken overdrive. There is no evil in my eight-legged friend, just hunger.

But in us . . . ah, that's different. I have known people who caught others in their webs, swathed them in silk, and sucked the juices from them. I have known people who would own and twist others to their own ends. I have known people who would do anything, anything, to others, would twist a whole life into agonized knots, rather than face their own inner insufficiency. This morning's paper has a story about child prostitution in Thailand, in which it's clear that layer upon layer of society colludes in hurting and exploiting these children, often infecting them with AIDS, while choosing quite deliberately to be blind to the effects of its choice on these children as individual human beings. To maim a child's life so men can have a few seconds' spasmodic pleasure . . . That is a choice for which these individuals will be answerable to God.

Spiders are merely spiders. But we human souls—and we are souls, every single one of however many billion of us there are today—are not hard-wired to treat another human soul as an "it" to be used and exploited. Ultimately, whatever our rationalizations, we have no real excuse. We may be predisposed to such cruelty by the way we have been treated by life. Culture may go against God's values. If we've been treated evilly or brought up lovelessly, we may choose to inflict on others what we ourselves suffered. And God knows, there are monsters in this life . . . But always, always, we have the choice to return good for evil, to choose love over destruction—every one of us, even the monsters.

I have watched those who put themselves and their own needs at the center of the universe, seeing others only in relationship to themselves: "To the extent that you meet my needs, you are an acceptable person; if you fail to meet my needs you are bad and a failure, but in my eyes, you don't exist as a real, live, separate person with feelings and needs of your own." The sad thing, ultimately, is how tiring this becomes, how ultimately unsatisfying. It takes more and more energy to resist the call of Love. The spirit collapses under the weight of this massive egotism. In the end, these are such sad souls.

It's one thing for the spider to treat the moth as an "it," a thing, not as a moth totally unlike any other moth and therefore precious in God's sight. The spider is not biologically capable of doing otherwise. Spiders are hard-wired to eat moths. They have no choice in the matter. But we have choices. I can choose to buy cheap clothing made by exploited Third World labor. When the soldier, hysterically possessed by hate, raises the machete and brings it down on human flesh, he makes a choice. When the husband sinks a fist into his wife's belly, he makes a choice. When an adult uses a child for sexual gratification, he or she makes a choice. When the toy soldiers, full of self-righteous rage, create a bomb to take a revenge that to them is oddly fictional but to their victims is very real, they make a choice. And they inflict their choice on innocent lives.

This, it seems to me, is the real Problem of Evil. How, in the face of such overwhelming evidence that God is Love, that we are called to live in loving relation with others, can anyone choose to turn his or her back and walk so resolutely in the other direction? I'm not sure it's childhood trauma. It may be that these individuals, never having received real love in infancy, have never really developed the receptors for it. I don't know. I don't understand, and I probably never will. I can only know that God allows us to choose, and suffers profoundly when we choose to walk away, when a soul chooses its own will over God's and insists on that choice over and over and over again, turning its back on the Light and running headlong into Darkness, as God cries out in agony and longing.

But don't ascribe evil to spiders. My friend in the window is innocent, except of living.

The Hand of the Potter

Babies

When I was a girl (back in the late Cretaceous), Christmas, for me, was a time when the space-time continuum warped somehow and Mystery bent down to brush the face of the earth. I did not, do not, have the language to embody or pin down what Mystery was; I could hear it musically, and I could see it as deep blue shot with silver. But I knew (although I didn't know how I knew) that during the darkness of Christmas night, you could feel it brush the world like a moth's wing.

Then I fell away from faith. Years later I became a mother, and now my image of Christmas is dual, divided, unintegrated, because one side of me still senses Mystery's moth-wing, while the other half sees the Nativity in very practical, motherly terms. Christ is no longer only the Embodied Godhead or whatever. He's a baby. I know babies.

From experience I now know his downy head, with the leathery soft spot where the bones haven't joined. I know the weight of him, the warmth, the peculiar feel of a newborn, how the head fits into the hollow of my collarbone. I know that his whole arm from elbow to fist is the same length as my thumb. His feet are tiny; his fists, with their tapering fingers tightly curled but ready to grasp an adult finger, are the size of large almonds. My hand can cover his back, easily. His eyes are dark and unfocused; his face has the squished look of newborns; his legs are crooked from the shape of the womb, and he is dusky-red. Held in the crook of my arm, he turns his head, instinctively rooting for the breast.

From this greater knowledge I can feel for Mary, in her pain and exhaustion and exhilaration and bewilderment, and let's leave all the physical stuff out of the discussion, because it's messy. I can feel for Joseph, too, exhausted by onlooking, unsure of himself in this new role, with the woman who is his and the child who is not his, but who, I think, he probably took into his own heart. I still can't do the shepherds and angels and wise men and all that, though. Not in my experience.

I cannot yet reconcile the moth-wing of Mystery with the physical immediacy of the baby. Not the Christ Child, not the Infant Redeemer, not the plump, insipid toddler outheld like a bowling ball by legions of remote Artistic Madonnas. The moth-wing is real; there is that something, that divinity; "angels bending near the earth," a star-shot blue immensity with huge significance in its folds. The newborn was (is?) also very real, and there is nothing more vulnerable, needier, noisier, plainer, or more human than a newborn. You put them together; I can't. It's some consolation that theologians have argued for a couple of thousand years about the divine nature and the human nature of Christ.

At least I'm not the only person who can't figure this out. But then, I'm not sure that I'm supposed to do that. Perhaps I'm expected to do only two things at Christmas: to listen for the wing brushing and to cuddle the kid.

Wall Fall Down

Robert Frost's grave is in my hometown, and I used to go and sit by it when I was a girl. In his poem "Mending Wall" he wrote:

> Something there is that doesn't love a wall,
> That sends the frozen-ground-swell under it,
> And spills the upper boulders in the sun . . .

The frost is coming out of the ground right now, and it is buckling roads and tumbling down stone walls and wrong-angling the cedar-post fences that zigzag through this mud-season landscape. Forces underground are heaving rocks up into the soft, heavy clay soil, to clunk against the harrow's teeth. New warmth sinks into the big rivers—the Rideau, the Ottawa, the St. Lawrence—and the ice buckles and churns up in chaos, which we try every year to manage and control. Not always successfully.

God forbid we should let the walls be breached. What would happen then? Compartmentalize. It's so much safer that way. The wall tumbles? Build it up again, higher and stronger.

> And on a day we meet to walk the line
> And set the wall between us once again.
> We keep the wall between us as we go,
> To each the boulders that have fallen to each.

God forbid we should let our walls be broken. We spend so much energy walling off parts of ourselves from ourselves. How can I live with that old pain, which will tear me apart if I release it? How can I live with me and what I've done? How can I live with being so much less than I think I should be? We spend so much energy walling ourselves off from others. How can I live with being seen, and seen truly, as imperfect and needy and human, wanting love so much and being so terribly afraid of it? We spend so much energy walling ourselves off from God, looking for any excuse not to face straight into God's deep insight and total love.

God forbid we should let ourselves be broken. We are (God help us!) so all-fired fearful of being poor, ordinary, hurting, imperfect sinners. That's where the walls come from, the source of our rigidity—from that, and from the world's cruelty, which has taught us to be fearful and has hurt us so badly. And we end up so distorted as a result of our fear, so rigid and lonely, so far from grace, acting in ways that only make it all so much worse, cutting ourselves off from love and health and freedom.

Then comes Jesus, looking straight into huge pain, humiliation, injustice, betrayal, staring at it hard, during that moment in Gethsemani, and then bending his very strong will to God's and accepting it all. Points himself straight into agony, like a boat pointing its prow straight into the storm. In total, radical trust, he allows himself to be broken.

The world says, "If it ain't broke, don't fix it." Jesus, mad as a hatter to the bitter end, says, "We can't be fixed until we're broken." And shows us, by his practical example, what happens when we let God be God and release ourselves into God's hand, not dodging the breaking moment but taking it trustfully. And in that shattering moment, the two of them, Father and Son, break brokenness itself.

The warm, strong force of the Resurrection—God's powerfully, terrifyingly *alive* love breaking through and sinking into us, as the new year's warmth sinks into this thawing land and water. It swells up under our walls, breaking and tumbling them, as the earth's swell breaks and tumbles a stone wall. We are cracked open, gently if that's what God knows we need, less gently perhaps if we're tougher nuts, because it is indeed "the crack in everything" that lets the Light get in.

And then, when we're broken and helpless as babies once again, we find ourselves being tenderly held and released into a new softness and gentleness and trust, where we can be free and loving once more, and truly, resiliently strong, no longer rigid. Paradoxically, the more we allow ourselves to be broken, the more whole we become; the more we allow the walls to tumble, the more we find how little we really needed them. The more we die, the more alive we become. The more we trust, the less reason we have to be fearful.

> Something there is that doesn't love a wall
> That wants it down.

Praise God.

Tearing Up the Scenery

I have an old house. It's about a century old, and it has been extensively mucked about with. It has great bred-in grace, phenomenal woodwork, and a sort of cheerful and comforting spirit to it. People tend to unwind here. They relax and the tension goes out of them. And that's the house's doing, its spirit.

It needs all sorts of work. The house itself is sound and well built, and nothing's structurally wrong—except, of course, for the trivial fact that the entire back half slopes roughly six inches over fifteen feet, but that's just the way it is, and we've all learned to live with it. But it's like a fine table that's gone without tending and has been neglected and misused. It needs a new finish, applied with love.

There was a moment, back last fall, when I recklessly ripped up a bit of horrible old carpet in my room, and that first step has set this whole process in motion. I have taught myself to patch plaster, and I've ripped down old wallpaper and torn up old carpets. I did my own room first in sage-green and ivory, showing off the graceful bay window with lace curtains; and I have just finished another bedroom in apricot and cream. Bit by bit I'm getting there, one room at a time.

But the process, ah the process . . . the process is a delight and despair to me, an exuberance of accomplishment and learning and a slough of exhaustion and stress, beauty arising out of complete chaos. If this house is to shine again, we're in for some Interesting Times.

Somehow everything else has to get done, and does get done more or less—my children get fed, laundry gets folded, I meet my deadlines (give or take a day), my domestic arrangements slide toward, but never quite over the edge into, total squalor. But while I'm in Renovation Mode, what really drives me is the state of the plaster. I rejoice over a stripped wall in good condition. I despair when I prod at a little crack and a good part of a ceiling falls down. I am owned by the process for the duration, and God help anyone who gets under my feet.

Nor is it possible to stop once I've started. A room can't be half renovated and left; if I'm to use the room—and each part of my house is too important to be *hors de combat* for long—it has to get *done*. So in Renovation Mode, I am possessed by the process, not in possession of it. So, too, does God in us, of course. As Martin Smith puts it,

> It is unnerving to reckon with a life active and powerful at work in the most intimate core of our beings with access to inner rooms from which our own conscious minds are barred. One of the signs then that the truth of the Spirit's presence is beginning to make itself known is that we feel as if, in Paul Claudel's colorful words, "an undesired lodger has moved in, one who does not hesitate to rearrange the chairs according to his taste, to drive nails into the walls and, if necessary, even to saw up the furniture when he is cold and needs a fire." The truth of the Spirit's indwelling is incompatible with my sense of autonomy, my complete ownership of myself.

If we give God the slightest opening, some corner of the Spirit gets lodged in us like a splinter in the skin; or some old corner of toughened hide gets lifted and the Spirit slips in—an infection of health. That's where the process starts, as my renovations started when I pulled up that bit of carpet.

But my house doesn't have to agree to what I'm doing to it; it is a house, whereas I am a living soul. God requires my consent, not once but time and time again. I have to keep agreeing to this inner spiritual renovation, saying, "Yes, Lord; I trust you; get on with the next bit." Because, in fact, the process can be pure hell. The pain can be tremendous as the old bonds are loosened. We go through chaos. We're racked by the fever of healing, our lives torn apart by the process of becoming and changing and growing toward something.

The Spirit is tugging us, urging us, nudging us toward exposing that particular, highly individual, one-of-a-kind beauty of soul that God sees latent in each and every one of us. Always, always, the Spirit calls to our own inner selves saying, "Please let me love you." And we must respond in trust.

If we're willing to get on with it, to face into and ride the pain through, and to live with the chaos, trusting in God's purpose for us, then we emerge with a new fullness of soul, a new responsiveness, an ability to love truly and deeply, to be fully free and fully human. Our souls' colors are richer and deeper, more beautiful, more honest.

My house's real, individual, very personal beauty, veiled by years of neglect, shines out when I rip apart with care and rebuild with love. I mean to do all I can to bring that beauty forward. But I know that God is doing to me what I am doing to my house; and if sometimes the process of soul-making seems messy and chaotic, well, I've agreed to that, in trust. I know from my own experience in renovation that the process can be hellish, but in the end the beauty is worth what it costs.

The Spirit expects us to step out into the process, to "let go and let God," in deep trust that we're obeying the One who built us in the first place.

Blessed be the Comforter, who can be so very uncomfortable.

-9-

Outward and Visible

The Church

I had forgotten how beautiful it was: the good proportions, ample but not overblown, the detailing done with thoughtful and loving care but without ostentation. The beautiful, deep polish on the woodwork, the slate floor, the huge and handsome windows. I had forgotten how I felt when I'd first come to it, as a child of ten, with that sense of recognition and homecoming. I'd forgotten how it had been as much home as the houses I'd lived in. I'd forgotten how intimately I knew it, every inch. There was the window with the six-fingered angel. There was the white marble font. The choir stalls, the white marble mosaic chancel floor, the steps I'd sat on, the pulpit my father preached from—all set aside from my life for years, and still as known and unconsciously familiar as my own hand. Everything in it was rich both with real beauty and with deep association. I had forgotten but it was all there, almost exactly as I'd left it, back before the whole world changed.

I'd been mistaken, I realized, in turning my back on all this years ago. Not on faith; that had been an ember in the ashes all along. But I'd turned my back on church, on much of the beauty and richness of life. I'd fallen into the trap of a sort of puritan utilitarianism, and in so doing, I'd sliced off a major piece of life.

I can see the positive side of this attitude. It says that we should focus on the liturgy of worship, not the worship of liturgy. It insists on practicality and intellectual honesty, and those, too, are good things. It says, rightly, that ultimately the least of the hungry, even the worst of humankind, is worth infinitely more in God's eyes than the handsomest cathedral. But carried to extremes, given no rein or balance, it's the same impulse that strips out so much of beauty and relatedness from life and leaves us soul-starved, disconnected, restless, and unhappy, longing for . . . something. There's a mean, denying streak in our heritage that, in the name of the plain, austere, pragmatic, provable, anti-materialistic, simply kicks beauty apart for the sheer hell of it. Or, when it says "Things don't matter," it is really saying "I can't be bothered."

People are hungry for spirituality, we hear; but they're also hungry for this richness, this sense of ceremony and ongoingness, a sense that not everything is modular and disposable. Martha Stewart taps into a deep desire for it. Yeats wrote, "how but in custom and in ceremony / Are innocence and beauty born?" and it's those things that we both reject, in angry hurt, as being unattainable and still long for as unattainable. This longing can easily slide over into a sort of Bridesheadian Toryism, but beneath it lies something real. That the longing can turn in the wrong direction, like any other longing, does not make it any less real, any less important.

People are, perhaps, in search of a something that I first discovered as a child in this particular building, which for me is instinct with whatever-it-is—"an unsatisfied desire which is itself more desirable than any other satisfaction." C. S. Lewis calls it Joy and separates it sharply from mere Happiness. It is an intense sense of, and longing for, something that we can only sniff, and see out of the corner of our eye, and hear a whisper of, but which is there, brushing a wing against the world. The suspicion of God. The possibility of Love.

We're wrong to strip beauty from *this* life, to see *this* life only as a sort of athletic training for the next. We're wrong to see things or human connections or human love as being somehow mere disposables, always replaceable. In this, as in much else, perhaps our ancestors were wiser than we are, insisting that the service of God should be as beautiful as we can make it, that we should push our talents to their furthest, making the best that we can make, being connected, rejoicing in creation and in each other, to God's glory and in thanksgiving.

God is in *this* world, instinct, drawing us to himself. The whole of this particular building, the mass of its broad stone structure, sits on this world's breast, grounding faith in the here-and-now, while we hearken for the yet-to-come. It sits on its ancient piece of ground like a child's weight on the knee, tying abstract love to the sheer loveliness of the living—a loveliness we should embrace and revel in, knowing that it (and we) will die, and we will have to mourn it and be mourned in our own turn. Love is not yet to come—it's here. Christ taught us that. We can turn away from Love, or we can walk straight into its arms, as I walked into this church's arms as a child and again as a middle-aged woman, come home.

Back in my home church, the church that to me will always be like a beloved nurse, I found a pew and prayed for a bit, and struggled with the sense that the past and the present were colliding. It felt like two ends of a broken bone being brought sharply together. For a few minutes, surrounded and flooded over with Love, fighting the tears down because I was afraid that if I started I wouldn't be able to stop, I wasn't sure I could stay or would have to flee. I stayed. The prodigal, come home.

Crosses

It spends each night on top of a scented candle in a green glass candleholder on an overturned splint basket, next to my bed. And so when I pick it up each morning and slip the heavy silver chain over my head, it is, briefly, redolent of the candle's fragrance.

While I was renovating my room last fall, I found a pretty, silk-lined, antique trinket box that I'd bought years ago and forgotten long since in the rough dailiness of life. In it were things I'd also forgotten long since, small treasures from the lost long-ago, living in protective neglect on the back of a closet shelf. A charm bracelet from my teens, a rather grubby, small wooden doll in a faded handmade blue satin dress, a locket, a broken watch, a penknife, this silver Celtic cross. My mother gave it to my father, who gave it to me.

It's a powerfully handsome thing, a cross for St. Patrick's hymn, big and almost too much "in yer face, mac!" for city wear. This cross is very strong meat. But it's also a real beauty, boldly ornamented, full of incident. David and his harp, shepherds and sheep, the prodigal being embraced, two figures and a book (the Annunciation?), and in the center a child. Much of the content is mysterious, veiled. The artist (who was it? when?) who made the mold had in mind specific scenes which were full of deep meaning to him or her but which I can't fully understand. Are those four things laid out in a diagonal cross four seeds unfurling? And what's the tiny leaping animal in the circle right above the child's head? What is the child holding? It could be a very large flower; it could be a sponge on a reed; it could almost be a mallet or an axe. But none of this really matters. All will become clear in due course.

This is my fifth cross. One broke when knocked to the floor by an angry, disbelieving hand; two disappeared in interesting ways, and two I gave away in desperation. Crosses seem to come into my life and to exit on their own schedule, and I have learned to accept this procession of tiny crucifixes as being somehow right and proper. This one will be a part of my life for a while, probably not forever. It came to me from an unknown source, and sooner or later it will pass from my possession into the hands of another person. But for now—today, tomorrow, next week, next year—it belongs to me, or rather I belong to it, and that too is right. When it comes time for it to move on, another cross will appear.

Why this cross? Why now? What is the thing trying to say, in its way?

I've taken it off and set it down next to the keyboard, and I'm looking at it as I type. It speaks to me, this cross, of courage, of being bold and firm and trustful in faith. It speaks of living into the fullness of life. It speaks of deep grief and the willingness to endure that patiently, facing right into it without skimping, and of great joy and the willingness to accept and embrace it—to look into joy's face unblinking.

It warns against the littleness that takes refuge in self-satisfaction and narrowness and self-imposed restrictions. It warns against the deep dangers of numbness and unawareness. It cries out against cutting off parts of life out of fearfulness, of retreating into the least-possible-trouble. It speaks of entering fully, but also gently, into another soul's pain instead of standing to one side.

It insists on growth and change and the fullness of being. It holds out for truthfulness and honor and living each moment in the Way. It talks about pointing the soul's prow into the wave instead of scudding for shoal water. It has no use for fear, this cross; it talks about the willingness to step out into thin air, the willingness to love with the whole, unfettered heart, the willingness to endure and be strong.

I've slipped it back on, and for a second the chain is cold on the back of my neck. I'm not sure I can live up to this one, but the cross knows that too. The metal will warm up in a second, and for the rest of today the two of us will be together, it banging and thumping gently against my breast whenever I move, asking sometimes for me to hold it in my closed hand, keeping me company, holding me safe.

Part 4

The Dancing Ant

-10-

Living into Grace

Twirling in the Suet

I spent Friday picking over suet.

The women's group of our church produces several hundred Totally Authentic English Plum Puddings as a fundraiser each fall, and one of the Totally Authentic touches is that the puds are made with Real Beef Suet. The suet is my job, as a sort of pre-Lenten penance. So each fall I dutifully trot out to our friendly local slaughterhouse and come home, after the proper small-town chaffing and lots of secondhand smoke, with garbage bags of disgusting, warm beef kidney fat. This stuff has to be chilled to solidity and repeatedly cleaned (it takes three passes) before it can be chopped into faintly pinky-white, clean, light, fresh-smelling beadlets of beef suet, sixty pounds of the stuff, looking innocent as styrofoam, every bit.

After the first sort-through (which is revolting—trust me, you don't want to know), the work settles down into one of those pleasantly undemanding jobs that leave the mind free while keeping the hands busy, if rather greasy. I find work like this particularly good for reflection and prayer, which I call Martha-prayer, for Lazarus's busy sister. But above all, I find it valuable for letting my mind wander.

I used to feel guilty about the amount of time I spend in the mental equivalent of screensaver mode—most like the enchanting screensaver in which blocks of the screen shuffle rapidly but randomly around. I should be Cogitating. I should be Reading, Marking, and Inwardly Digesting. I should be Meditating. I should be Planning. I should be at least *thinking* instead of twirling in vague circles like flypaper dangling in the breeze.

Then, from talking to colleagues, I began to realize that writers all do this, and it's an important part of the process for us all. A certain amount of what Robertson Davies calls "creative lassitude" seems to be necessary. I find it easiest when those bad children, my senses, are preoccupied; otherwise they're like restive kids in church. If I hand them the equivalent of paper and crayons—say, suet to pick over and shred, or silver to polish (but not tidying, vacuuming, or taxes)—then they settle down and are quiet, and I can ignore them. This seems to be critical. I've never been able to ignore a crying child, and that goes for my senses too.

Among many other things, what emerged from this afternoon's dive into highly saturated fat and mental mushiness was that the mushiness (not the fat!) is God's way of working with my soul without my mind getting underfoot. I like to be rational and reasonable, and that means that I like to plan and control the process. If I do *this,* then logically *that* should follow; if I plan, if I change this or that, if I scheme, if I manipulate . . . and of course this sort of frantic mental activity is almost exactly the last thing I should be doing.

If I do the planning, I invariably screw up. Looking back through the years (all too many of 'em misspent or painful, or more usually both), I find that I am not, in fact, particularly good at running my own life. If I try to plan out a route meticulously, I invariably get lost. If I drive by the seat of my pants, I may get lost, but I invariably come round right in the end, even if sometimes I've spent time heading south when north was what I wanted.

If I let God and my subconscious tussle things out, while my mind shuffles little pieces of the screen around and my fingers are busy with something mechanical but mildly fascinating, like shredding congealed beef kidney fat, then things emerge, things I can't put a finger to, but they are definite directions, instincts, intuitions—the sense often of being nudged hard in a particular direction. It may be a very strange direction. It may, in fact, be a direction that seems inherently contradictory to all common sense, a 180-degree course correction from the course I want to take. Sometimes the ways involve a good deal of immediate personal difficulty or pain; sometimes they are easy and grateful. But when I have the sense of the Spirit telling me to jump *this* way, the only possible response is "How high?"

How can we tell this sort of vocation from our own inward impulses? By the fact that it's as apt to aim us in directions that we don't want as in directions that appeal to us. By the fact that it emerges oddly, with a sort of calm certainty: this way, not that way; but I can't explain why. We can always find rationalizations to do what we want to do or not to do what we don't want to do; we can't always rationalize what we're called to do or not to do. We may think we really know what we want and need, but we're apt to fall into our true God-called vocations like someone stepping backward, tripping over a log, and sitting down hard in a puddle—but it turns out later that it was the *right* puddle, the one you'd been looking for all along, but in all the wrong places.

Father-God and the Holy Spirit—the one emanent, the other immanent. One overarches, transcending; the other bathes our deepest taproots, washing them with nourishment, down there in the depths of unconsciousness, where the good work of healing and growth truly happens. Which part of a tree matters more, the crown or the root? Or the trunk that connects the two and makes them one? Silly question.

The two of them were at it again, conspiring, the one calling to the other, as my fingers teased the pure, creamy-white fat from its membranes and vessels and my mind floated quiet and still. Really good prayer is the Holy Spirit singing to God and God listening, and the job of my busy, controlling, competent mind is to shut up and get out of the way. True vocation grows from the deep darkness right out into the light, often in startling ways.

My mind's job is to find practical ways to carry out God's direction for me, not to decide what that direction is to be—nor to be turned off, for God gave us good, sensible minds to use, not to be treated like meatloaf. Still, my mind's job is implementation, not policy; policy is of God. That policy may not be what I thought I wanted and needed. But I'm learning to trust my soul and God to figure out what's best for me, and to listen to my instinct instead of my strong head's wish to get what I want, my own way, as quick as I can.

"To turn, turn, turn will be our delight / Till by turning and turning, we come round right." And if that means letting my mind twirl gently in the wind, then so be it. Hand me another bag of suet; we're not done yet.

Mud Season

It has been, bluntly, One of Those Days. We've had a steady downpour, washing away the last traces of summer. We are in for it now, "it" being winter as we do winter here (which is, thank God, not quite as they "do" winter in Winnipeg!).

But winter won't get properly underway for another five or six weeks or so, just as there's about the same hiatus at the other end, between the last serious snow and the first real green. You good folk south of the border may think of the Canadian winters as being tough, but trust me, they have NOTHING on Canadian mud season. Both of them, the fall and spring versions. Winter has a certain cheerful brutality here, but mud season is terribly hard on the spirit.

Mud season is grey. Mud season is sloppy. It is actually harder to stay warm in mud season than in full winter, because of the damp. Mud season is dispirited and dispiriting. Mud season makes people irritable. Mud season seems interminable. Mud season has no viable sports or occupations. Mud season (worst of all) keeps the kids indoors a whole lot.

It is, however, possible to see beauty anywhere if you're prepared to be open to it. I don't think it works if you actively *insist* on finding beauty; that's like Pollyanna saying, "I'm glad my leg is broken, glad, glad, glad!" That's reality denial, and our Lord does not ask us to deny reality. Only to be open to it.

So what has mud season got to offer us? Where is its beauty? In its quietness, I think. Maybe mud season has a certain contemplativeness. It's best approached in a meditative mood, one that looks at textures instead of colors, for while mud season is uniformly dun-colored, it's rich in texture—look at a ditch or patch of woods and see the sheer visual complexity.

Mud season is quiet. We're past the frenetic joys of the short (and buggy!) Canadian summer; we are awaiting the severe beauty that lies ahead. We are in stasis, just for now, while we prepare for what is to come.

Mud season is anticipatory, preparatory. The fall spell takes us through the gradual, gentle cool-down that nature needs to be ready to endure the Big Freeze without deep tissue damage. Spring mud season, on the other hand, is a time of enormous if unrecognized growth.

It is not a pretty season, this one. But it does have beauty and meaning, as does, of course, everything that leaves our Creator's loving hand.

South Wind

The wind is from the south tonight, very strong, and it's been raining all evening. I don't know if it's the weather that makes me so restless and unable to settle tonight or if it's life itself, which (as always!) is so much a mixture of things: tears in the morning, laughter and great delight in the afternoon, great hope and fear mingled . . .

I don't know how to center myself in prayer tonight. Oh, there's always supplication on others' behalf: pray for the situation in Nigeria, for those who are ill or in danger, "for all those who in this transitory life are in trouble, sorrow, sickness, or danger." I find tonight that the lips may move and the words may come (if not fluently), but the heart just won't stay at its business. The adoration and thanksgiving engines are also balking and sputtering. Contrition is usually my strongest suit, but tonight I can't even still myself long enough to feel guilty.

Maybe sometimes we are simply blown like leaves on the wind; or like leaves on the water, we are carried, apparently aimlessly. One great advantage of being somewhat . . . chronologically advantaged? . . . is that I'm beginning to discern that there is also a pattern to this apparent lostness, this seeming randomness—what has been called spiritual dryness. I may be least able and inclined to do my work as a Christian at times like this, although I find it's important to go on with the discipline of church and prayer and works. BUT it's in times like these, now that I look back, that God seems to be busiest with me.

I have learned the hard way on my journey that it's in these times of spiritual restlessness that I feel least close to God, because God is too busy shaping me to want to chat. It's as though God is down in my personal basement fiddling with the plumbing. Everyone knows that you let a good plumber get on with the plumbing, maybe bringing him a cup of coffee now and again but not interrupting for idle chat or getting underfoot. It's only when I look back that I realize that God's creative hand was busiest at its healing, transforming best when I was least aware of it.

Maybe this is terrible theology. I don't know. All I have to go on here is my experience: that peace and delight will come when

God has completed his latest renovation project. While the work is in progress, I am going to be unsettled and edgy, a prey to fits and starts, but then the hand of the Potter is firm on the clay.

Dance, Then . . .

It has been One of Those Weeks.

Never mind what happened; it's a long story. But to quote a friend, "Mother always said there'd be weeks like this, but she didn't say how many." Another friend simply says that life is Being Like That. It's been Being Like That since Sunday morning. By Friday noonish, when Bob-at-the-office asked me how I was doing, I found myself saying, "I'm vertical. You perhaps expected more?"

The details aren't important; what does matter is the pattern. Looking back, I can see that the week was a time of emptying. Emptying is a fine, old Christian tradition, following the path set by our Lord in the desert, in the garden, on the cross. But the process can be painful, and this time it was. Very. By Thursday night I was so purely strung out that I snarled quite seriously at a friend who'd poked a sore spot, purely by accident. He is a Christian and kindly forgave me. I may forgive me too, sooner or later.

What gets me through times like these is my children. I don't mean that in any sweetly maternal sense, <gack!> although I am deeply grateful that my younger one is still a lap cat. No, what keeps me going is the need to find a matching sock. Lunches have to be got. School forms must be signed and returned. Because our joint propensity for mess far outstrips even my generous tolerance, I have to do some tidying. There are the bills and groceries. And finally, there is the soft, endlessly flowing tide of laundry, giving life a quiet rhythm that sustains me when very little else does.

There are going to be times in any faithful life when faith itself goes phhhht, when there is a dark, faintly chilly, faintly musty space in the mind where faith and hope have their regular spots. Or the sensation could more resemble what happens when a back tooth loses a major filling—that sense of a hole that you could park a truck in and can't keep your tongue out of. Or the gap can be an active ache, or a deep uneasy numbness, as of something amputated—"There's a pain in the room somewhere." The symptoms vary, but they're all unnerving and rather miserable. It's not depression; you can still function and eat and sleep. But it's no fun, either.

There are various terms for this state of being. I like "Dark Night of the Soul," which has a certain panache. If you're going be this miserable, you might as well at least have the satisfaction of a little melodrama. Sometimes "the only way out of this [stuff] is straight through it, one step at a time," so you concentrate on where you're putting your feet and let the future care for itself. But after a while a person starts looking skyward and saying, "Okay, God, my character is strong enough; lay off already!" Or more quietly, "Oh God, where are you?"

How can one do this emptying process, these forty laps in the desert, and still manage to retain some joy, some optimism, some sense that "all will be well and all will be well and all manner of things shall be well"? I was thinking about this aloud, and it came to me—an image that I can hold on to for my own personal comfort, like a totem or stuffed bear.

God does not plan our lives, in the sense of making a blueprint that we're to follow. God is not a drill sergeant, expecting us to move in lockstep to a march by Sousa (although some people still seem to prefer to think of God that way). That image makes nonsense of free will and God's grace and pardon. But if we look up from our self-concentrated fearfulness, from studying our hands in our laps, as it were, we find God standing there, asking our company, waiting to lead us into the dance.

Now there's a thought to play with. Dance has a rhythm and a pattern to it. Because it flows and is flexible, it can allow such contingencies as luck, happenstance, natural disasters, the Problem of Evil. But it's a co-creation: God leading and setting the pattern, but we, far more than puppets or slaves, with our own worth and beauty in the pattern.

What could such a dance be on a practical level? It might be a monastic discipline. It might be a personal pattern of readings and prayer. It might be the rhythm of running a household and raising a family, if you're one for Martha-prayer. It might be a pattern of work and activity. It's whatever we're granted, whatever patterns our lives.

What the dance certainly is is a pattern of self-discipline, of minding manners and meeting necessary obligations, of holding your tongue sometimes and making yourself speak up at others.

It often fits Meyer's Law (in any emotionally difficult choice, the harder choice is probably the right one). It expects us to dance like adults, as gracefully as we can manage. It allows, sometimes, that we have not the health or strength to dance the dance to its fullest capacity. But it does also expect us to love it enough to dance to *our* fullest capacity, whatever that is.

Sometimes the music of the dance will bring light and happiness and laughter into our lives, or richness and warmth and deep satisfying colors, or even a quiet darkness shot through with silver. And the music will shift to meet our movements, and we will shift our movements to meet it, moving in its grace. Sometimes we will dance with a knot of others, sometimes with a particularly beloved partner. And sometimes, most preciously, we will be given the sense of truly dancing with God, feeling that tiny electric flow through the hair on the forearms.

But sometimes there is no music. Or the music is all discordance.

And sometimes there is no partner, much as we'd love to have one, or the beloved disappears, leaving us empty.

And sometimes there are no fellow dancers near, and we feel exposed and lonely and falter: where is everyone?

And sometimes it seems as though God has left the dance entirely, and there is no dance at all, only me, by myself, looking a complete idiot in this desolate empty room, with the dust motes floating in the wheylike light, and none of this makes any sense—was I dreaming? is it morning now? how could I have been so *stupid*?

So, what do I do then?

Keep on dancing.

Step through the pattern as I know it. Manage each step as I remember it, hearing the music in my head, humming it under my breath. Whisper the steps to myself: left, right, cross the toe over, turn, step forward . . . Keep my balance as best I can, try to keep my back straight and my chin up and to move with what grace I can muster. If I fall hard, then I must pick myself up, feeling like a perfect fool and aching abominably, rub my bruised dignity, cry a little, and get back into the pattern just as soon as I can.

If I can trust in nothing else, I can trust that what I do in the way of sock-hunting and lunch-making and floor-sweeping—the ordinary discipline that my kids' lives require—is a form of love: "Work is love made visible," as a sign on a levee over the swollen Mississippi said a few years ago. Maybe my dance is not as fine and handsome as monastic evensong, but it's what I seem to have been handed to step out, at least for now. I can trust this Martha-work to carry me somehow, even if my mind is full of confusion and darkness and the tumbling chaos of old pain. It will keep me going until my hand grasps Mary-faith again.

I can trust in the pattern of life, the swing of the seasons. Just as the milkweed lets fly its miraculous seeds again, as it did this time last year, so the dance circles. You may find yourself working through the same figure again, with similar partners, but this time—oh, such a difference! But it never precisely repeats, because the dance is directional, taking us somewhere. If we're quiet, we may perhaps hear faint sounds of other music, telling us where.

For now, I can trust that when I don't know what the next dance figure will be, I will be taken into and through it, so long as I'm willing to follow the lead. I may be called to dance alone; I may be called to dance with others. But I will know more as the dance unfolds. Above all, I must trust in God's skillful choreography, hard as that sometimes is for me to see as I crane my head, looking around for what lies ahead. What we'd all give for skywriting sometimes!

Even if this room feels cold and empty and achingly echoing, even if there seems to be no one here but me and the dust motes, I will trust and keep putting my feet in the patterns. I will trust that the music will come back, that the dancers will be there, that I will feel the Dancer's touch again. It will come. It will come.

Dance, then, wherever you may be . . .

(For AES)

The Journal

Way back there in the late Pleistocene, even before my long-ago youth, it used to be the custom that young men off at college would send their laundry home to their mothers, who would send it back all clean and starched and ironed. This laundry shuttle made use of a particular mailer—a brown, two-piece box, about the size of a small suitcase, with straps to close it and a slot for a card with the address. I acquired one of these boxes at some point, and for years it has been the Family Archives, stuffed full of oddments and records and whatnot. I had occasion to go through the Archives last week—through the photographs and the letters from high school friends, the notes from a beloved great-aunt (may Dodo rest in peace), the postcards, the locks of baby hair. I spent a long minute over one particular folderful of letters, recollecting a lost beloved face. I found the documents I wanted. And at the very bottom of the box was something I'd long since forgotten: a journal I'd kept during Interesting Times, some twenty-one years ago, a critical time of change in my life.

It was strange, looking over words which I do not remember writing but which are definitely mine. Strange seeing the raw data from which I have constructed my personal history. Strange being reminded of the sequence of events, of the feelings, of the players, even of the weather. Strange finding the photograph of a face I'd forgotten had once been my own. Strange being reminded of a self that is still me, and is yet not me at all anymore.

We have memory, but even in memory we're here in the here-and-now, ourselves as we are now. I can, for example, remember my children's infancy, but I can't go back to being the younger woman I was when they were born, any more than I could go on to be the woman I will be (if I am here) when they are adults. My memory is free to slide back and forth like a bead on a string, but I myself am locked in present time. Confronting another, earlier, stranger self, as I did reading my old journal, is a rather different experience than simply remembering.

If C. S. Lewis had it right, and I suspect he probably did, when we part company with this life, we will stand before God and see no longer the Godshadow we chatter on about, but the unimaginable Light itself. And God will, metaphorically speaking, gently take us by the shoulders and turn us around and make us face ourselves. And then we will *see* our whole selves, our whole lives from soup to nuts, all self-deception and pretension removed, all opened out and laid bare. We will see ourselves as God has seen us, and some of that will be pleasant, and some of it will not.

More, we'll each see how our life affected other lives, like a pebble dropped in a pond, the ripples spreading out—ripples intersecting other ripples, canceling, augmenting. We will understand all pain we've caused, all pleasure we've given. We will see the chances to love that we missed, the accidents that didn't kill us, how a chance turning aside changed a life, in ways that we could never have understood.

The process is apt to be painful. Becoming increasingly aware is always painful. So much sin results from our ducking that necessary pain and fighting with all our strength to remain ignorant, to stay in the womb of the nice, safe, easy Dark. No such luck. Ultimately, there's that Birth, and it will happen, fight it as we will. We can begin it in this life, or we can try to postpone it all till the next, but we *will* be born into true consciousness, and the Light will undoubtedly be hard on our eyes.

The important thing to remember then will be this: that while the Light may seem too bright and the new awareness may be as strange and frightening as the first touch of cool air on a newborn's skin, there will also be loving arms to wrap us close, enfolding us and holding us close to Love. For while God sees us, and we will eventually see ourselves, with painful clarity, God is also the one who is to us "like those who lift infants to their cheeks" (Hosea 11:4), treasuring us in joy and delight.

I liked the girl in the journal, the young self I'd forgotten. She was nicer than I remembered, a sensitive and loving soul, struggling to make her choices responsibly and well and keeping others' needs in mind. But there were also passages in that journal that made me wince, because she could claw like a cat, that one. She'd been long in pain, and the pain had made her angry, closed off and wary, over-controlled, and self-defeating. "We have met the enemy and he is us," as Pogo said. I'm hoping that in the end, that first self will prevail and will be the one to stand before her Maker. But I'd be a fool to deny that the dark self exists or that I am not answerable for her (my!) actions.

We have to keep facing into the Light, turning away from the easy Dark, walking into and through the fire, accepting the pain, the burden of awareness and care. But with the pain comes a deeper, richer sense of life, real joy, a new intensity of being and loving.

We have to walk this road hoping that in this life we will begin to become what God is calling us so urgently to become: the fullness of who we are, the best we can make of our gifts of nature and nurture and choice. We have to aim for all this, so that when God has turned us around to face ourselves, at last meeting our own eyes and seeing clearly our own faces, we will at least be able to smile through our tears.

On Hold

At last the ice is gone, the bitter weather has broken, and it's possible to get out for long country walks again.

It may be a little early to declare Spring Mud Season officially open, but we're close, I think. This is the other of the two annual inter-season seasons in which it gets ugly around here (the other Mud Season is between autumn and winter). We have thawed on a massive scale; the creek is choked with greeny-brown ice and is swollen and churning. All stands revealed that was decently cloaked for the duration: lost mittens, cigarette butts, dog droppings, waterlogged advertising supplements, decomposing leaves. This under a heavy sky that can't quite make up its mind whether to rain, mizzle, or merely befog.

Funny thing, though, it may look ugly out here, but to my countrywoman's eyes, it's not at all gloomy, properly looked at. What to me is gloomy is the glossy hyper-urban shopping center where I spent a couple of hours last night—the groomed and handsome people with their blank faces and unseeing eyes, each in a private universe, unconnected. Of course, they're Real People too and souls beloved by God, but they still scare me back to the boonies every time. I can't cope with that sleekness. It may be messy out here in this scruffy landscape with its cedar bogs, but I find the grottiness oddly comforting.

It's real life: when the pure, white, softening, frozen blanket of easy certainty melts away under Christ's warm and steady gaze, we are usually left facing a bit of a mess. When we stop lying to ourselves, clutching our cheap self-regard to our chests like a blankie, we realize that we really are Miserable Offenders:

> Saints know what God wants;
> I don't know what God wants;
> I think I'll stick with the sinners.

As my favorite theologian rightly points out, repentance is a result of forgiveness, not a cause. We can truly accept ourselves as Miserable Offenders only *after* we've accepted ourselves as beloved by God. Until that happens, we can't afford to look at ourselves that closely. First the snow has to melt. Then we can face what's underneath it.

God takes away our self-regard, our easy answers, our crutches and excuses; God strips away the veneer we cover ourselves with, to show us what lies beneath. Turning us to the mirror, holding us secure, but begging us just to *look,* God shows us us, warts and droops and love handles and all, and shows us also that we are astonishingly beloved and beautiful in our Lover's eyes, if we will only allow ourselves to be.

It's process, not a one-time-only thing. We may be in the early stages of spring Mud Season now, but we'll get winter back now and again in the next month, as well as the odd day that speaks of true spring. It may be ugly out here, grotty and grey and disheveled, but even as I write, the sap is rising; the skin-of-the-earth is stirring in her sleep. And I know what beauty is to come.

Swallowing Faith

Driving today through western Massachusetts, south of my particularly favorite mountains, listening to tapes that I'm used to from my very different landscape in the cedar swamps, and feeling life coming together like two eyes converging.

I don't have my Penguin Book of Modern Verse here (it's on the window sill next to the computer at home), but it has Robert Frost's "Two Tramps in Mudtime," which ends, I remember, with:

> But yield who will to their separation
> My object in living is to unite
> My avocation and my vocation
> As my two eyes make one in sight.
> Only when love and need are one
> And the work is play for mortal stakes
> Is the deed ever really done
> For Heaven and the future's sakes.

Things pulling together, a wholeness, a unity. Jackie, the person who's been a cybersister for months, is embodied being and I'm sitting in her apartment, at her computer, writing this, while she and Marlene get supper and their baby black Lab, the Divine Miss B., tries to eat my skirt. I knew these beings too were "real," but the realities have drawn together, have coalesced.

Living into grace is a matter of making two realities come together: belief and life. I wish it were a one-step process, but certainly for me it isn't. Belief is so easy, a matter of intellectual consent. I may fight a little, but I'm generally willing to yield. A God who could so casually engender a galaxy, a milkweed pod, could certainly manage a fertilized egg without benefit of human sperm. A God whose force, in all its subtlety, can arrange the millions of precisely engineered cell divisions and specializations needed for embryogenesis—such a God can manage the miracle of a resurrection. No sweat.

But then there's the small matter of getting this belief business down from my head into the rest of me. Belief stays in the head too easily, for the heart and the gut are more stubborn sites. So much of what ails us, what separates us from God and one another, lies in our viscera—not literally, of course, but in our deeper reaches. Belief seems to get stuck at the larynx, uncomfortably, a bit of dry bread that tickles, a husk that makes us cough, not a nourishing or comforting food for the whole of us. It only seems to get past that point a tiny bit at a time. Worse still, it's the areas where we need faith, real faith, the most where we have the most trouble finding it—the areas closest to our hearts, things like love and work and our children and the future. Here belief sticks like a Parkinsonian patient, frozen in mid-move.

Somehow I must learn, in even the most tender parts of my life (the ones I'd much rather not have God looking at at all, thank you!), that belief and life can, in fact, unite; that together they make faith—the willingness simply to take the rest on trust, at the deepest level, serenely letting go and letting God, stopping the need to clutch and control.

Maybe for others it's simpler; I don't know. For many of us, it does seem to be a becoming-thing, not a being-thing, a slow coming together, not the blinding knock-you-off-your-donkey flash of brilliance. Slowly the convergence, the gradual trust, the slow movement of belief down into our darknesses and depths, God granting us what God knows we can afford, when we can afford to receive it.

Peace

The path cuts across an abandoned field, from a dirt road near my house to out behind the town's one and only mall. I like walking out that way, not just because of the wildlife (at the moment, black-eyed Susans, Queen Anne's lace, and a gazillion tiny frogs that jump practically under a person's sneakers), but also because that particular small patch of creation has a quality of intent quietness. There are no sounds there but whatever the Earth is speaking to herself, and she's usually a quiet lady.

The quietness is more than mere absence of noise, however. I could find mere silence in any number of places, from my basement to the nearest church. In fact, the path is full of birdsong and crickets' buzzing. What the path does have is a *living* quietness— not the quietness of stone but the quietness of growing and being things. For all its apparent peace, this is a place where life and death and copulation and hunting and hatching and seed-making and pod-maturing are all in progress, and living things are about their ways in a world I barely notice as I walk. There may be equilibrium here, but there is no stasis. This is a place of fullest life.

It's that quality of living quietness that draws me, steadies me, comforts me, as no cloister silence could. I find myself heading out to the path whenever life has decided to get Very, Very Interesting, because the quietness draws grief out like venom from a snakebite. This is a very safe place to cry, this path, because its very quietness is somehow deeply companionable. You can be angry or in pain, and the living quiet takes the anger or pain into itself and quiets you and brings you back to balance and peace.

"The first duty of love is to listen," Paul Tillich said. I find I'm not always very good at listening, and I don't always feel listened to either. I find sometimes that I'm thinking more about what I'm going to say when the other person stops talking, and only my sense of courtesy keeps me from interrupting. Or I find the solution to whatever-it-is so obvious—if the person would just do this or that, the problem would disappear. Or I have my own internal preoccupations that I'm bursting to talk about, or my list of things that Must Be Done or the world will end. Or the other person is complaining about X? You think X is a problem? Let me tell you about Y. Or sometimes it's simply that I haven't talked to another living adult human being in three days and I desperately need to babble myself for a while instead of paying careful attention.

But I've also had enough experience of being on the receiving end of non-listening to know better. I know how it feels to be shut up by another person's failure to receive what I need to be free to say. And once, just once, I was on the receiving end of real listening by a first-rate pastor, who set his own problems aside to listen to me, drawing me out, and I know what peace and healing that brought.

We talk about the Peace of God, but I don't know that I've ever heard a definition of it that made sense to me on a gut level. Maybe what we call the Peace of God is God's simply listening to us, receiving us as and where we are, in quiet, companionable love. Maybe the intensely living quietness I find on the path is the closest I can come to God's peace, at least today, in the confused and buzzing here-and-now.

Maybe I should stop struggling to create peace inside my own confused and buzzing self, with its huge, unresolvable contradictions of faith and faithlessness, hope and despair, flashes of joy and pain. Maybe instead I should simply let God's companionable quietness suck all the turmoil out.

But how could I do that? Can I at least try to release my tight, controlling grasp on what most roils my own internal waters? Maybe I'm not supposed to wrestle *every* angel to the mat. Maybe I'm supposed to lie back in God's arms, chattering to God like a child instead of pretending to be the grown-up I know in my heart I'm not.

To have the freedom and safety to trust truly, to be received, to be loved and heard and tended—given what we believe, given what we say about God and faith and life—then why, for God's sake, do we find it so very hard to take all this, which is what God so badly wants to give us?

-11-

The Spinner

Anonymous Miracles

Was talking with a friend, and the question came up: Why don't we ever think of God's grace as being graceful?

We'd been discussing serendipity—the blissful accidentalness of things, Godincidences, the way, for example, God sometimes seems to work on the Internet, times when in apparent chaos and accidentalness God gets particularly (and sometimes most sneakily!) busy in our lives, sometimes with stunning and wholly unexpected results.

Sometimes, looking back, we can see some sort of pattern— almost a playfulness, it seems to me—when we "let go and let God" and allow a measure of chaos or unpredictability in our lives. When we're in the tightest control is when things seem to work least well. When, for example, I'm trying to find my way home and I'm worried about getting lost, I'm often best off simply putting myself on autopilot and letting some instinct, some inner magnet, guide me home.

I'm not suggesting that we be irresponsible or foolish, that we not exercise ordinary common sense. But sometimes we have those instincts—that sense of a hand pushing us sharply between the shoulder blades—that makes us take chances, to open our lives to something less predictable. Sometimes if we give chaos some room to play in our lives, interesting, even profoundly positive, things result. It's when, for example, we get into cyberspace, where accidents abound and grace, perhaps, can play quite freely, that cybercommunity can form. Maybe the element of playfulness, of randomness and chaos, is one of the richest things that the Internet can give us. Maybe that says something about church too?

I don't know. I'm just guessing. But I do wonder . . .

Hanging Out the Wash

Today, for the first time this year, the weather was fine and mild enough to hang the laundry out. So I spent the morning washing and filling the line with sheets—there is nothing like air-dried bedding, one of life's greater minor pleasures. For once, instead of seeing all the yardwork which needs to be done and which I don't think I can possibly accomplish singlehandedly, I let myself fall into Martha-prayer, the contemplation possible when the hands are busy and the mind is free.

It has been almost six months since I last stood out here flinging sheets on the line and nipping on the clothespins. And in that time my life has been so totally transformed, so radically rewritten, that, looking back, the change takes my breath away. So much has taken on such new meaning, such new life. Just an example: these sheets, the dark-green ones bought back in November, stand for a breakthrough in my own self-view, a winning through to healing and wholeness and new life and love. These sheets weren't even here the last time I hung laundry out to dry; this is their first turn on the line.

And my sons' blankets—the kids, too, have been transformed in the last six months as we've formed our new family. It hasn't been easy for them, but they have grown and matured. The older one has begun to say hello to his adult self; the younger one has finally begun to say goodbye to his baby edition. For them, too, this has been transforming time. They too have grown in grace and faith.

As I pin out the pillowcases, I'm listening on my mental radio to music memorized from a hauntingly beautiful CD I just got: two strong, supple women's voices singing "Shall we gather at the river," while down at the foot of my field I can see the creek, ebullient and quick, flashing light in the new sun, rushing in fullness and power. This time six months ago the creek was a stagnant trickle and these sisters-in-the-spirit of mine were only strangers.

Now it feels as though we are indeed gathered at the river—the river of grace and life, of joy and new peace, as we have formed cybercommunity in love in the last while. A community that has nourished me root and crown in these months, and that I now love as family in Christ.

The sky is broad and deeply blue; I've always thought, "This is the blue that chocolate would be if chocolate were blue." While it's still mud season (hey, this is Canada, and it's only March!), I can sense the grass stirring under last fall's matted leavings. The twigends on my three huge maples have begun to swell. A fresh wind from the southeast whips the sheets around, snapping them, but not too roughly.

I have learned, since I last stood here, to do only what I can do today and to trust God for the rest, and the more trust I have given God, the more reason I have been given to trust even more deeply, in every area of my life.

Six months ago I was called to step out of my old life (which was a form of death) into what felt like empty air. I did so, and God's grace caught and upheld me. I think I am finally learning to fly.

None of it's my doing; I know that. All this comes through the grace of God, through the strong love written so powerfully in the events we will be remembering and celebrating in the next week. We have the bridge from sin to grace, from randomness to deep meaning, from death-in-life to a new quickening, from lost-aloneness to included love, and it is given us in a great clap of breaking pain on the Cross. Such a huge act of love is something that we could never, in our wildest imaginings, have asked for, but the love is given to us, time and again. We can do nothing to deserve this. We can only be stunned by God's sheer prodigal grace.

Paradox and Orthodox

I am looking at a piece of crewel yarn.

It is lying on the oak dining room table, where I work at my embroidery and listen to my tapes. It is a deep, bright blue-green, the color of a male mallard's head, deep peacock blue. It was expensive, this skein, because this is the very finest long-staple pure wool, a strong yarn, a remarkably even yarn, as thin as it can be for the finest effects—a yarn that I can keep dragging stitch by stitch through the twilled cotton fabric on which I'm shaping my wreath of fancied flowers, without the strand disintegrating as ordinary wool yarn would.

I can take my working needle and pull this strand apart. It is two-ply yarn; that is, two fine-spun single strands have been twirled together to form it. With the tip of my needle I can nudge these strands apart, tease them into separation, gently pulling them to unspin their interdependency, and then . . . dissolution. I find myself with two weak, wavering, fuzzy threads, neither of which can be threaded through a needle's eye, much less used in my embroidery.

So it is that paradox is stronger than orthodox. Alloys are stronger than pure metals, and then there's crossbred vigor. Change and stability, rules and freedom, sacred and profane, male and female, health and weakness, sinfulness and optimism, faith and works, honesty and love . . . I could go on for several pages here. We need both strands; neither alone is strong enough. It's the union that makes for strength and fineness and the ability to be genuinely used.

A good friend boasts of his strength and stability and resistance to change: "I am who I am." Friends surfeit their daughter on praise and love; she never hears the word "No." A father tries to toughen his son through yelling and punishment. We resist ALL change; we accept ALL change. All these are (fundamentally) the lazy way out. We make blanket rules, hold on to simple patterns and behavior, in the slothful avoidance of actually having to think. Black-and-white is so much easier than the constrained uncertainty of grey.

Life is two-stranded always, always a matter of walking along the peak of the roof, with a slippery slope to either side of us.

Sometimes it's right to be kind and accepting, sometimes it's right to administer a swift kick in the name of love; sometimes it's right to hold to the old, sometimes it's right to let go and reach for the new—and each decision, if we're doing this right, is no easy one, and is made in love for the other.

It's those last two qualities that allow us to live in paradox, that spin our two strands together, to take the difficult path of honesty, and to operate in love. Nothing else will do. Love without the astringency of honesty is a weak, sugary broth, and honesty without the sweetness of real love is a bitter brew.

I pick up the strand of deep peacock-blue yarn and thread my needle, and begin to shape the next flower, whipping through the drum-tight cloth, confident that this fine, thin, even, strong yarn, so much stronger than its two interspun plies, will hold out till the end of my work.

The Dancing Ant

It couldn't be deader-looking out there. The landscape looks flattened by the intensity of the cold that grips us. There's a smattering of snow, but not enough for beauty. This is worrisome weather for pipes and pumps, but more for people. Who will die on the streets tonight in this bitter weather?

January was not a good month for me, not by a long shot. Never mind why, but this evening, as I sat at a piece of crewel embroidery and listened to a tape, I have to confess that I felt as flattened and unalive as the landscape. Sometimes it looks so much simpler to be frozen. So I was musing and feeling thoroughly sorry for myself when the miracle happened. Okay, it was a very small miracle, but still . . .

I keep my crewel yarns roughly skeined and piled in a small wicker basket by my working lamp—a rather disorderly heap, but full of color. And round the topmost polished wicker of the basket an ant was marching—no, not marching; more like dancing. That ant whipped round that basket most purposefully, and then, sighting a strand of dark rose yarn, it fairly leapt aboard.

I watched, fascinated, as the little black thing danced among my yarns: from dark rose to middle-violet, to marigold, to deep turquoise, to leaf green, to dark green, to light rose, to deep violet, from swirl to strand and shade to shade the ant ran, rapidly, randomly, seemingly confident and even happy, if an ant can be those things.

Of course, that's anthropomorphic on my part, and ants can't see colors (and can we see the colors God sees?), but still . . . It came to me that there is necessary grief, necessary sorrow, and it's wrong to shirk those. But the wise man also said that there is a time to mourn and a time to put away mourning, and maybe the time had come to put away mourning. That's what the ant was saying, if God is up for using ants to make a spiritual point, which wouldn't surprise me in the least.

We can choose to live lifelessly, grey as this frozen landscape, and that is safe. And it is also dead, because, as chaos theory points out, equilibrium for a living system is death. Or we can choose to be alive, to welcome chaos and color, risk and richness, loss and love—to run, as the ant did, leaping confidently among the deep colors.

I cannot literally dance among the strands of bright yarn as the ant did, but I can dance in my mind in the sheer glory of God and of God's love for me, in the sure and certain knowledge that "tears abide for an evening, but joy comes in the morning."

Women in the Kitchen

Two women working in a kitchen, talking of love.

The kitchen is messy; one woman is tidying and doing dishes while the other starts the evening stew. We are sisterly enough to move around each other well, handing a spoon, sweeping crumbs off the table, not getting under each other's feet. Our combined broods (three of her boys and my two) are playing quietly. We have these conversations often, work together often; this is comfortable for us both.

We are both used to Martha-prayer, the contemplation possible when the hands are busy, and to Mary-talk, the talk that ranges happily in the realm of the Spirit, inquiring, trying to discern, sometimes (we sense it) going astray, but always coming back to this: What is God's pattern in our lives? What is God's direction for us? Where are we called? Who are we meant to become?

We are talking about making our souls. We both feel called in particular directions, with particular people, and we sense (although we don't always know) that these vocations are God-directed. We can sense, perhaps, a purpose, a directedness about these callings, for ourselves and others. We have no sense that God is skywriting for us, but if we look sideways over our shoulders, we can glimpse a sort of pattern out of the corner of our eye. God would never exploit us, but we have long since given God permission to use us, and we sense that that, perhaps, is exactly what's going on.

We are talking about love—and no, I won't say what kind of love we were talking about or what situations we were discussing. We both refuse, almost fiercely, to set any boundary between the divine and the everyday, between the sacred and the secular. God is not set apart; God is instinct, inherent, in every atom. Love is not sacred or erotic, brotherly or parental, marital or friendly. It is merely love, taking in the whole person, undivided—God's intent for us, a calling. To be for another person God's love with the human skin on.

Not an easy choice or a cheap one. My friend is called to help a beloved soul reach toward its completion, sensing that her role in his life is eventually to help him out of life itself; we know that he's beginning to fail. I am called in a different direction, one with its pain as well as its joys. This is not cute hearts-and-flowers stuff we're talking about, and it has a price.

It's dancelike, our talk, as the light starts to go and the dusk flows in blue over the snowy fields; and the theme of our dance is the glory of God, in its gentleness and splendor, its deep intent and infinite reach.

God be thanked for all those to whom we are linked in love.

The Spinner

Now that the end of the school year is in sight (from summer holidays as a working single parent, dear Lord in your mercy, deliver me!) it's field-trip time. On Tuesday my younger son, John-of-the-bee-brown-eyes, duly trotted off with the rest of Mrs. Caldwell's Grade 4 class for a tour of our local agricultural college. Among other goodies, he brought back a small plastic bag with a fistful of raw sheep's wool.

Way back there in a previous existence, I learned to spin. Never mind why; like so many of my dafter decisions, it seemed like a reasonable idea at the time. So, showing John, I teased the fibers apart, lined them up, and then drew them out, twisting them into yarn.

He was bored out of his mind, of course. After he'd departed in search of better, less psychologically correct amusement (cap guns), I sat down at the kitchen table with the rest of the wool, playing with it and letting my mind wander.

You can clean wool quickly and roughly and efficiently by washing it in detergents that strip the lanolin out and combing it with mechanical carders. Or you can clean wool slowly and gently and inefficiently by teasing the matted fibers apart with your fingertips and letting the dirt fall out. Gently, because tearing at it only rips the fibers and makes for a weaker yarn. The strongest yarn results from thoughtful and careful treatment.

Musing on this and other matters, I played with the wool, teasing it from hand to hand. Some of the roughest, dirtiest bits I laid aside to throw out, but there were batches of soft, almost clean, short-staple underwool, soft as silk, crimped and shining ivory, lovely to the touch. I'd forgotten the feel of this stuff, and what it does to your hands—all that lanolin.

When I finished teasing the wool, the mass was cleaner, much cleaner, but not really *clean,* and I was still in the mood to muse, so I went at it again, loosening the fibers further, letting more dust fall onto the tabletop. I went through the process three times, and when I was done, the wool was a soft, light, airy mass, cream-colored, only slightly flecked with dirt. I put it back in its bag to show John.

I swept up the little pile of dirt—quite innocuous now—and picked up the dirtiest bits of wool, the ones I thought weren't worth trying to clean. Even as I started to throw the filthy wool away, I noticed that it included quite a lot of wool that might, just possibly, be salvageable. These hanks had to be handled a little less gently, but in the end I think I managed to get all the wool out of them and into the bag with the rest. In the end all I threw out was dirt.

If I'd been engaged in real spinning, I would have carded the cleaned wool into rollags with my carding combs. I would have cupped each rollag in my palm, drawing out the fibers between my fingers while the twirling spindle sent the necessary spin creeping up the strand—not too fast!—twisting it into yarn; and then I would let the yarn twirl down onto the spindle. I would have done this with a gentle, rhythmic back-and-forth of the hand, controlling the motion by feel—the whole motion as unconsciously wise and ancient and natural as settling the child on the hip to be carried. And then I would have skeined and washed my yarn and hung it to dry in the sun.

If I were a dyer, I could brew up dyes, from old wisdom and knowledge and what came to hand to color the stuff—indigo for blue, cochineal shells for scarlet, the skins of onions for deep caramel yellow. If I were a weaver, I could stretch my warp and shuttle my weft and pattern my colored yarns into a web. If I were a clever tailor, I could cut and shape and stitch that bright web into garments that a dancer might wear, making creative use of whatever I'd been given to work with. If I were the Dance-maker, I could see all this, from embryo lamb to dancer, and I could pattern the Dance . . .

When my body fails me and I die, I think I (my soul, that is) will be like that wool after maybe the second or third time I teased it apart with my fingers—still a muddled, confused mass, still full of dust and slightly greasy, anything but white and pure and dryly perfect, but (I hope) not quite so full of sticks and burrs and sheep dung as it was originally. I will be a lot airier and looser and softer than I had been. I hope by then I may have worked most of the knots out.

But I'll still be in need of a whole lot more work most likely. God alone knows what beauty God—by spinning, dyeing, weaving, cutting, shaping, stitching, creating the dancers, designing the Dance—will make of me after that, in the Life I can only dimly sense but long for with all my heart.

I'll bet God's hands are soft, though. Spinners' hands are soft. Lanolin, all that lanolin.

> Glory to God
> whose power working in us
> can do infinitely more
> than we can ask or imagine.
> Glory to God from generation to generation,
> in the church and in Christ Jesus,
> forever and ever.
> Amen.

Source Notes

Epigraph: Deborah Griffin Bly, "Where You Are," from *God Help Us*. Compact disc. (Harrisburg, Pa.: Morehouse Publishing, 1996).

Pages 88–89: excerpts from "Mending Wall," by Robert Frost, in Oscar Williams, ed., *The Pocket Book of Modern Verse* (New York: Washington Square Press/Pocket Books, 1972) 178–179.

Page 91: Martin L. Smith, *A Season for the Spirit: Readings for the Days of Lent* (Cambridge, Mass.: Cowley Publications, 1991) 19.

Page 118: from "Two Tramps in Mudtime," by Robert Frost, in Oscar Williams, ed., *The Pocket Book of Modern Verse* (New York: Washington Square Press/Pocket Books, 1972) 181–182.

Page 134: "Glory to God . . ." General synod of the Anglican Church of Canada, *The Book of Alternative Services* (Toronto: Anglican Book Center, 1985) 214.